Also by David Carradine and David Nakahara

David Carradine's Tai Chi Workout:
The Beginner's Program for a Healthier
Mind and Body

David Carradine's Introduction

to

Chi Kung

The Beginner's Program for
Physical, Emotional, and Spiritual
Well-being

David Carradine and
David Nakahara

David Carradine's Introduction

to

Chi Kung

An Owl Book

Henry Holt and Company
New York

Advice to the Reader

Before following any exercise advice or the program contained in this book, it is recommended that you consult your doctor if you suffer from any health problems or special conditions or are in any doubt as to its suitability.

Henry Holt and Company, Inc.
Publishers since 1866
115 West 18th Street
New York, New York 10011

Henry Holt® is a registered
trademark of Henry Holt and Company, Inc.

Published in Canada by Fitzhenry & Whiteside Ltd.,
195 Allstate Parkway, Markham, Ontario L3R 4T8.

Library of Congress Cataloging-in-Publication Data
Carradine, David.
    [Introduction to chi kung]
    David Carradine's introduction to chi kung: the beginner's
program for physical, emotional, and spiritual well-being /
David Carradine and David Nakahara.—1st Owl Books ed.
        p.   cm.
    "An Owl book."
    Includes bibliographical references.
    ISBN 0-8050-5100-7 (pb : alk. paper)
    1. Ch'i kung. I. Nakahara, David. II. Title.
RA781.8.C37   1997   97-16271
613.7' 1—dc21

Henry Holt books are available for special promotions
and premiums. For details contact: Director, Special Markets.

First Edition 1997

Book designer: Betty Lew
Illustrations by Sarah Griffin
Technical Advisor: Arnold Tayam
Photographer: Mike Lamont
Models: Elizabeth Wright and Arnold Tayam

Printed in the United States of America
All first editions are printed on acid-free paper. ∞

10   9   8   7   6   5   4   3   2   1

Contents

Introduction　3

What Is Chi Kung?　　　　　　　　　　5
How to Use This Book　　　　　　　　7
History of Chi Kung　　　　　　　　　9

The Chi Kung Program　11

Assessing Your Self-awareness　　　　13
Philosophy of Training　　　　　　　18
The Plan　　　　　　　　　　　　　20
The Six-Month Program　　　　　　　24
The Three Regulations　　　　　　　26

Month One—Stillness and Movement　29

Still Meditation　　　　　　　　　　33
Stretching the Back　　　　　　　　　39
Opening the Gates　　　　　　　　　45

Month Two—Emptying and Filling　51

Cleansing Exercises　　　　　　　　　55
The Small Orbit Exercise　　　　　　60

Month Three—Building   65

The Five Element Exercises   70

Month Four—Purifying   85

The Five Element Personality Types   87
The Healing Sounds   97

Specific Ailments   105

Kidney Energy Imbalances and Solutions   *110*
Liver Energy Imbalances and Solutions   *114*
Heart Energy Imbalances and Solutions   *118*
Spleen Energy Imbalances and Solutions   *121*
Lung Energy Imbalances and Solutions   *125*
Energy Points   *134*

Month Five—Integration   141

The Seas of Energy Exercises   *146*

Month Six—Awareness   153

Heavenly Energy Meditation   *157*
Loving Kindness Meditation   *162*
Tools for Healthy Living   *166*

Recommended Reading, Viewing, and Listening   *167*
Future Plans   *171*
Biographies   *173*

THE SIX-MONTH PROGRAM

Exercise	Page #	Month 1	Month 2	Month 3	Month 4	Month 5	Month 6
Still Meditation	33	X	X	X	X	X	X
Stretching the Back	39	X	X	X	X	X	X
Opening the Gates	45	X	X	X	X	X	X
Cleansing Exercises	55	X	X	X	X	X	X
Small Orbit Exercise	60	X	X	X	X	X	X
Five Element Exercises	70			X	X	X	X
Healing Sounds	97				X	X	
Specific Ailments	105				X		
Seas of Energy Exercises	146					X	X
Heavenly Energy Meditation	157						X
Loving Kindness Meditation	162						X

David Carradine's Introduction

to

Chi Kung

Introduction

What Is Chi Kung?

Given our hectic way of life, I have always searched for the most effective, efficient, fully encompassing, simplest, and easiest way to maintain well-being. The Western disciplines are good, physically, but they do not always involve development of the mind and sometimes fail to offer the internal benefits that are needed for total health. Kung fu develops the mind and the body, but the training is not always easy; it can be especially difficult for the elderly or sick. Tai Chi is effective, efficient, and easy on the body, but it is not as simple as it could be.

My search led me to Chi Kung, a five-thousand-year-old art that is a necessary and practical way to manage the demands on our health. "Chi Kung" literally means "energy skill." It is the forerunner of Tai Chi. It is the health and healing aspect of Tai Chi, or, conversely, it is Tai Chi without the fighting influence. So effective are its therapeutic powers that today in China Chi Kung is used to cure numerous ailments, such as arthritis, digestive problems, sexual impotence, asthma, weight gain, and even cancer. Chi Kung is incredibly straightforward and efficient. There is no wasted motion or effort. Every ounce of effort is used to rejuvenate and restore energy and health in the body. Chi Kung is holistic. Not only do the exercises strengthen the body and clear the mind; they can also expel negative emotions such as worry, anger, fear, and sorrow from the body. Chi Kung is specific. There are Chi Kung exercises that restore energy and vitality in a specific internal organ, thereby isolating and maximizing self-healing. Chi Kung is simple and easy to learn. The exercises are, for the most part, basic single-movement calisthenics with a Tai Chi–like consciousness and flair. Chi Kung is not physically taxing. Many of the exercises were designed for the very ill. Some can be done lying down; all of them can be done sitting down. If you can breathe, you can do Chi Kung.

Chi Kung is based on the principle of internal energy flow within the body. This internal energy called "chi" exists in the body in a series of rivers, pools, and seas that nourish us and give us life. A person's health and well-being are determined by the flow, volume, cleanliness, and quality of this internal energy. The Chinese believe that all aspects of a person, be they physical, mental, emotional, or spiritual, are components of chi. After all, everything in the universe, whether animate or inanimate, solid or gaseous, is just energy vibrating at different frequencies. The Chi Kung masters discovered that this chi could be controlled and developed, affecting our total being. Not only could the physical self be healed by influencing the chi, but so could the psychological, emotional, mental, and spiritual selves—in other words, one could use Chi Kung to grow and mature as a person. The ancient masters developed exercises for cultivating the chi that involved deep breathing, visualization, movement, body structure, emotional cleansing, and meditation. To many, Chi Kung meant "empowerment," whereby one could directly and dramatically improve health and well-being. For me, Chi Kung means "hope," because I believe it can help me become the person I want to be.

How to Use This Book

This book serves a dual purpose. It can be used for dealing directly with a pain or illness, or it can be used as a holistic self-development program. There are many ailments that we suffer from that fall between the cracks of Western diagnosis. A condition may be caused by an energy anomaly that has not yet manifested physiologically but is nevertheless real. For example, a person may have a perfect physical exam every year for twenty years straight, and then one year, out of the blue, the person is diagnosed with cancer or some other devastating illness. From an energy perspective, this cancer could have manifested long before. It may have been avoided by cleansing and clearing the body energetically with Chi Kung. There are also ailments that are not severe enough to warrant a doctor's visit, medication, or surgery but that are still quite discomforting—conditions such as insomnia, lower back pain, fatigue, and headaches. This book approaches health problems from an energy perspective and gives you exercises that will help deal with your condition. If you suffer from a specific ailment, then immediately start with the "Specific Ailments" part of this book.

Energy stagnation that causes illness is often washed away or prevented by intensifying the overall energy flow within the body—what this program is all about. The process of developing energy actually involves a combination of physical fitness and inner searching. This means nurturing self-awareness, stilling the mind, moving the body, emptying yourself of bad energy and filling yourself with clean energy, building energy in the organs, purifying your emotions, integrating the mind and body, and expanding awareness. By working through this program you may find out a lot about yourself, things you never considered. This is the nature of energy development or any self-development program. However, whereas many self-development programs rely only on intellectual understanding, which can quickly fade away, this program teaches a physical exercise that reinforces and actualizes a philosophical concept. *The understanding does not come from thinking but from doing.*

History of Chi Kung

These things from ancient times arise from one:
The sky is whole and clear.
The earth is whole and firm.
The spirit is whole and strong.
The valley is whole and full.
The ten thousand things are whole and alive.
Kings and lords are whole, and the country is upright.
All these are in virtue of wholeness.

—Lao Tsu

In the beginning, more than 5000 years ago, the ancients looked to nature for wisdom and inspiration. They observed that the functioning of their bodies seemed to be in flux according to the powers of nature. They could feel subtle energy cycles occurring within them, flowing as if their bodies had their own internal ecosystems. They realized that this energy flowed naturally and unobstructed and changed as nature changed. As society grew more complex, confusion arose. People became disconnected from nature. Their internal energy flow became distorted and unnatural. The need to reestablish this connection with nature became apparent. The ancients felt that this disconnectedness manifested itself and/or was caused by a sort of heaviness and muddledness of mind and spirit. They began to meditate. Their goal was to become so mentally and spiritually light, clear, and expansive that they would blend, melt, and dissolve into the "void" or universe. They would become "one" with nature again.

As the centuries passed and as society continued to exert even more influence on people's lives, the ancients found that this return to nature was the work of a lifetime. Most would die before their mission was accomplished. To enhance the probability of reaching enlightenment, they began to place importance on preservation of the body. They combined very simple calisthenics, meditation, and breathing techniques to create exercise sets. The exercises were aptly called Chi Kung, which means "energy skill." So effective were these routines that even the terminally ill and the weak could regain their health and vigor. The ancients also found that Chi Kung could be used for therapy and treatment. They could actually project and transfer energy through their hands into another body, thereby inducing healing in the recipient. Conversely, they could extract negative energy from a sick body, thereby restoring health and the natural flow of chi. To the outsider the very idea seemed bizarre; to the ancients it only seemed natural. As the needs for reestablishing balance grew, Chi Kung became more sophisticated and merged with Chinese medical theory. Chi Kung soon became a powerful healing art and health system.

Centuries later the great fighters and martial artists experimented with Chi Kung as a way to augment their strength and power. Iron Body, Light Body, Crushing Palm, and other training disciplines were developed from Chi Kung. Masters of these arts learned to withstand heavy blows from mallets and spears and suffer no harm. Some could walk on eggshells without breaking them. Others could break rocks with a casual slap. So impressed and astounded were the martial artists that whole systems were created to incorporate these techniques. Chi Kung melded with Shaolin martial arts to form Tai Chi Chang. Taoist circle walking blended with kung fu to create Pa Kua Chang. Every martial arts system in China was enhanced and influenced by Chi Kung.

Today, generally speaking, Chi Kung is divided into three schools: martial, medical, and spiritual. The beauty of the martial Chi Kung routines is the sheer power and vitality they offer. The medical Chi Kung exercises are therapeutic, concentrated, and specific, providing solutions for pain and disease. The spiritual Chi Kung sets are soothing, bringing peace to those who practice and seek it. Although all three schools have their unique offerings, all of them were used for inner searching and expanding awareness. They challenged people to reach inside themselves to extract the gifts that are available to all of us.

The Chi Kung Program

ASSESSING YOUR SELF-AWARENESS

The truly great man dwells on what is real and
not on what is on the surface,
On the fruit and not the flower.
Therefore accept the one and reject the other.
—Lao Tsu

A major component of Chi Kung training is self-awareness. Understanding who you are—your strengths, weaknesses, fears, attitudes, and aspirations—is very important to achieving and maintaining health. Chi Kung training is not just physical exercise and circulating energy; it is learning to feel and perceive. It is understanding your mind and body. It is embarking on an inner search for your true self. This is the true power of Chi Kung. Tapping into the energy is merely a vehicle or guide or bridge to take you deeper and deeper into your consciousness, subconscious, physical body, emotions, personality, memories, fears, false images, or, simply, your total being.

We are all born perfect, innocent, and beautiful, capable of wondrous things. Yet as we grow up we accumulate experiences that are so painful that we choose to build walls and barriers to hide our wounds. We develop false images of our-selves to cover our vulnerabilities and overcompensate for our weaknesses. We muddle and suppress the genius and talent that exist within us all. Our energy system is directly inhibited by how fiercely we hold on to our false images. Conversely, our energetic strength is enhanced by how easily we let go of our masks and veils. "Letting go" is accomplished by seeking truth within yourself. The truth can be painful, temporarily, but it can also be liberating. Be as honest with yourself as possible, because without truth improvement is impossible.

Answering the questionnaire is the first step to getting in touch with your body, your state of health, and the quality of your life. It is also a way to break down barriers of self-denial that inhibit the flow of the body's energy. The effects of Chi Kung can be subtle but profound. Your day-to-day progress may be barely discernible, but your improvement over a period of a month or two can be quite dramatic. The following questions will help reveal your present condition. Answer them quickly and briefly. One-word answers are best. It is recommended that you photocopy the questions and write your answers on the photocopied page. Put it away in a safe place, and then, later in the program, we will ask that you revisit your responses. At that point you will realize how powerful and fully encompassing Chi Kung really is.

SELF-AWARENESS QUESTIONNAIRE

DO YOU BELIEVE THAT YOU WILL SUFFER IF YOU DO A BAD DEED?

DO YOU FEEL GOOD HELPING A STRANGER?

DO YOU GET ANGRY WITH SOMEONE AFTER IT IS TOO LATE TO RESPOND?

DO YOU WAKE UP LOOKING FORWARD TO THE DAY?

CAN YOU ENJOY BEING ALONE?

DO YOU GET HEADACHES?

DO YOU EAT WHEN YOU ARE EMOTIONALLY DISTRAUGHT?

DO YOU EAT WHEN YOU ARE NOT HUNGRY?

DO YOU EAT FOR TASTE *AND* HEALTH?

DO YOU EAT A LOT OF FAST FOOD?

DO YOU EAT A LOT OF FROZEN FOOD?

DO YOU EVER REGRET THAT YOU DID NOT EXPRESS YOURSELF?

IS THERE SOMEONE IN YOUR LIFE YOU BLAME FOR KEEPING YOU FROM BEING HAPPY?

DO YOU BLAME OTHERS FOR YOUR FAILURES?

DO YOU FEEL SUPERIOR TO SOME PEOPLE?

DO YOU FEEL INFERIOR TO SOME PEOPLE?

DO YOU ENCOURAGE PEOPLE TOWARD SUCCESS?

DO YOUR FRIENDS GENUINELY SUPPORT YOU IN YOUR ENDEAVORS?

DO YOU ENJOY SEEING OTHER PEOPLE FIND HAPPINESS?

IS WINNING EVERYTHING TO YOU?

IS AN EQUAL DEAL A GOOD DEAL?

DO YOU HOLD GRUDGES?

DO YOU LET PROBLEMS GET BIGGER BY NOT DEALING WITH THEM?

IS IT DIFFICULT FOR YOU TO CONFRONT PEOPLE?

DO YOU FREQUENTLY GET ANGRY WHEN DRIVING, OR AT OTHER TIMES WITH LITTLE PROVOCATION?

DO YOU LAUGH AT YOURSELF?

DO YOU STAY MAD AT YOURSELF?

IS MONEY THE ANSWER TO ALL YOUR PROBLEMS?

IS MORE BETTER?

DO YOU VALUE EXERCISE?

DO YOU VALUE REST?

ARE YOU MOVED BY BEAUTY?

DO YOU NEED PRAISE?

DO YOU LIKE TO LEARN?

CAN YOU BE SUCCESSFUL WITHOUT HARD WORK?

ARE YOU AFRAID OF HARD WORK?

IS IT OKAY TO BE WRONG IN FRONT OF OTHER PEOPLE?

CAN YOU ADMIT YOU WERE WRONG?

CAN YOU APOLOGIZE IF YOU WERE ONLY HALF WRONG?

IS APOLOGIZING THE ANSWER TO YOUR PROBLEMS?

IS YOUR WAY THE ONLY WAY?

DO YOU LITTER?

DO YOU WORRY ABOUT THINGS YOU CAN'T CONTROL?

DO YOU SEE THE GOOD IN PEOPLE?

DO YOU FIXATE ON THE BAD IN PEOPLE?

ARE YOU AFRAID TO LOSE?

ARE YOU AFRAID OF SUCCESS?

ARE YOU AFRAID OF BEING REJECTED?

ARE YOU AFRAID TO BE A BEGINNER?

ARE YOU AFRAID OF CHANGE?

DO YOU BLAME YOUR PARENTS FOR YOUR FAULTS?

DO YOU FINISH WHAT YOU STARTED?

ARE YOUR BEST YEARS AHEAD OF YOU?

CAN YOU FORGIVE?

DO YOU PLAN FOR THE FUTURE?

DO YOU ENJOY WHAT YOU ARE DOING?

ARE YOU THANKFUL FOR WHAT YOU HAVE?

ARE YOU DOING WHAT YOU DO BEST?

ARE YOU NOT DOING WHAT YOU COULD BE EXCELLENT AT?

HAS YOUR ANGER RUINED A RELATIONSHIP?

IS YOUR ANGER RUINING A RELATIONSHIP?

ARE YOU AFRAID TO BE ALONE?

Do you need to impress others?

Is your ego easily bruised?

Do you feel other people's pain?

Do you judge and condemn people?

Can you learn something from anyone?

Do you believe you have to give to get?

Is your life controlled by another?

Do you reflect on your life?

Do you consider consequences that don't directly affect yourself?

Can you read without falling asleep?

Do you mind having to walk to get somewhere?

Do you sleep well?

Do you hate anyone?

Do you love someone?

Do you cry?

Are you ever in awe?

Can you win gracefully?

Can you lose gracefully?

Do you like silence?

$\mathcal{P}$HILOSOPHY OF TRAINING

It is not wise to rush about.
Controlling the breath causes strain.
If too much energy is used, exhaustion follows.
This is not the way of Tao.
Whatever is contrary to Tao will not last long.
—Lao Tsu

Jerry Alan Johnson, a longtime Chi Kung and internal martial arts master, reflected back to the time when he first started training with his teacher:

> *I asked my teacher, "How long before I can become very good with the chi, the energy?"*
> *My teacher replied, "Three years."*
> *I was surprised. "Three years?! Well, what if I try really, really hard?"*
> *He answered, "Then it will take you ten years."*

The requirements for Chi Kung training are different from those of purely physical regimens. Qualities such as forcefulness, intensity, an ability to work through a high pain threshold, and the ability to push yourself to the limit are harmful. Attributes such as being undeniable, determined, and goal-oriented are good but can be counterproductive if taken too far. The ability to relax and feel, to trust in your intuition, and to be patient are the traits most valued. The energy needs to be coaxed gently and not forced by sheer determination. If you force things, you could hurt yourself with the energy. If you work through pain and exhaustion, you are denying the body's safety signals. If you try too hard and expect too much, this will bring on stress and tension in the mind and body. The energy will not flow if the mind is overactive and the muscles are tight. The energy flows when the mind is at ease and the body is relaxed. The more you relax, the more you will feel. The more you feel, the more you can control and cultivate the energy. The energy is very subtle. There are times when you will need to use your intuition to feel and sense the effects of the energy. The more you respect your intuition, the sharper your intuition will be and the more sensitive you will become. Also, your intuition will guide you to exercises that are better and more appropriate for you. Have patience with the training. There are people who get dramatic results within days, and others who feel very little after several months. Self-development is like growing a fruit tree. The growth of a fruit tree is invisible to the human eye, yet one day it bears fruit.

THE PLAN

As we mentioned, the ancient Taoists saw the energy of the body as an internal ecosystem with real characteristics and controllable tendencies. If this internal ecosystem is kept clean, vibrant, and flowing, the physical body will stay strong and healthy. The plan set forth in this book is designed to systematically achieve this state of health.

Imagine seeing a great piece of land hosting a network of rivers, lakes, seas, forests, and mountains. See the shape of the land as similar to the outline of a body. If the rivers are clogged, the lakes are filled with debris, the seas are polluted, the trees are brown, the mountains are deteriorating, and the air is filled with smog—you have the image of a diseased and unhealthy body. For most of us, our bodies are neither purely clean nor disastrously polluted, but for all of us, the body can never be too healthy.

To repair the land we must be able to see what we are doing. If we work on the land through a blanket of smog, we are working in the dark. The first exercise taught is Still Meditation. This exercise allows us to get "into our bodies." We can then start to feel, see, and sense our muscles, bones, posture, organs, physical functioning, emotions, intellect, intuitions, desires, fears, and all the things that influence our energy. Meditation increases our sensitivity and awareness while removing the blinding smog from our internal ecosystem.

Once we have a clearer picture of our own internal ecosystem, we must begin to unclog the rivers of energy. There are two main rivers that feed the entire system of rivers, lakes, and seas—the "conceptional" and "governing" meridians. We must remove the large clogs that pinch the flow of these main rivers. Through "stretching the back" we can remove tension along the spine where one of the main rivers of energy flows. Working out the tightness and tension will unkink the spine and restore the energy flow in the important Governing meridian. Since our sensitivity will have increased from the Still Meditation, we will feel where we are tight, tense, and sore and be able to concentrate directly on our weak points.

There are other areas in the body where the energy tends to stagnate, causing the rivers of energy to pinch off. Most commonly, these are the main joints of the body, referred to as the "Gates of the Body." Energy circulation can be restored and increased by warming, stretching, and opening these joints or gates. Stretching the back and spine is like bulldozing blockages in the Mississippi River. Opening the Gates is analogous to clearing impediments that are clogging the smaller rivers that run off the Mississippi River.

While stretching will remove the tension and tightness that pinches off chi flow, there are other factors that impede energy circulation. The river pathways in our internal ecosystem can be clear, but the water itself may be polluted and include chi blockages. These blockages accumulate from mental and physical tension. Through bouncing and shaking the body, exhaling the breath, and releasing tension in the mind, we can shake loose and expel negative energy. The "Cleansing Exercises" will purge stagnant, heavy, negative, and excess energy from the body and its rivers of energy. The energy or the actual water of our ecosystem will also be literally cleansed.

Once the pathways are cleared and the energy is cleansed, it is time to directly intensify the flow of energy. This is achieved by a simple physical and mental exercise called the "Small Orbit Exercise." The Small Orbit Exercise increases the circulation of energy in the two main rivers, the Conceptional and Governing meridians, which make up the "Microcosmic Orbit." All the rivers of energy flow through the Microcosmic Orbit at some point. It is the Mississippi River of our ecosystem. Increasing the flow in the Microcosmic Orbit will affect and eventually flow over into the other energy pathways of the body, thereby strengthening the entire system.

In our internal ecosystem there are also pools or lakes of energy that are connected to the rivers of energy. These lakes are analogous to the Great Lakes in that their influence and size are significant. There are five primary lakes, and each one is located and associated with a main internal organ, namely the kidneys, liver, heart, spleen, and lungs. These organs are collectively called the "five Yin organs." When a person has an illness associated with one of these organs, it is often attributed to an excess or lack of energy in the lake of energy associated with that particular internal organ. The imbalance is usually caused by a blockage in the river that feeds into or drains out of the lake of energy. The "Five Element Exercises" are designed to balance the chi flow in the five internal organs. Whereas the Small Orbit Exercise works on the internal ecosystem as a whole, each of the Five Element Exercises concentrates on a specific set of problems.

Vibrancy and health in the five Yin organs can also be attained by "purifying" the energy of each organ or the lake of energy associated with the organ. This is achieved by doing the "Healing Sounds Exercises," which vibrate the organs with sound. This vibration will shake loose and dispel stagnant and negative energy that tends to exist in these lakes of energy. This negative energy usually stems from supressed emotions. By doing the Healing Sounds Exercises not only are you clearing away bad energy; you are also releasing negative emotions.

The Five Element Exercises and the Healing Sounds Exercises can be used to combat specific negative conditions, or they can serve as a regular health maintenance routine. The "Specific Ailments" section (page 105), while not part of the daily program, gives additional solutions for certain conditions. This section uses a combination of self-acupressure and self-massage techniques to stimulate the rivers and lakes of energy. Acupressure involves applying pressure to a specific point along a river of energy in order to stimulate chi flow. Self-massage is designed to heat and activate energy in targeted areas, usually in regions of multiple acupressure points, physically tense areas, and in the lakes of energy that house the organs.

At this point in the program you will have learned how to open and cleanse the rivers and lakes of your ecosystem. You will have the necessary tools to thoroughly revitalize the body. However, it is still possible to deepen the healing process even further. There are three "Seas of Energy" that serve as receptacles or storage areas of energy. All of the rivers of energy flow into these seas either directly or indirectly. The lakes of energy intersect and connect with the seas. Physically these seas are centered deep inside the body. The "Seas of Energy Exercises" heat, stir, and circulate the energy within these seas. Because the seas have depth, the effects can be profound. One can vastly change for the better physically, emotionally, and spiritually from practicing these exercises. The Seas of Energy Exercises are placed later in the program because their effectiveness is influenced by the cleanliness and vibrancy of the rest of the ecosystem. If the water that pours into the seas from the rivers and lakes is polluted, then circulating the energy in the seas is still beneficial but not optimal.

At this point in the program the landscape of your ecosystem should be healthy and fertile. However, no man is an island. The energetic makeup of a person needs to mesh with its surroundings. The "Heavenly Energy Meditation" energetically connects a person with the "Heavenly" energy from the cosmos while establishing an energetic connection with the earth. This meditation also connects the three Seas of Energy into one great ocean. Internal martial artists use the energetic connection with the earth for additional power and stability. Energetic healers conduct the Heavenly energy into their patients to initiate a rejuvenation process. The Heavenly Energy Meditation is a step in developing these abilities. In our ecosystem the Heavenly Energy Meditation is like creating rain to add quantity and freshness to our energetic environment.

If a person is healthy and possesses a great deal of energy, it does not necessarily mean that this person is a good person. Without the negative energy and physical and emotional pain that can distort a person, it should be easier for all of us to be just and moral. However, selflessness and generosity does not necessarily result from being strong, vibrant, and healthy. The "Loving Kindness Meditation" teaches one to be compassionate and universally loving. In our ecosystem we can have a healthy jungle that is dangerous or a healthy utopia that is good for all. The Loving Kindness Meditation is designed to be beneficial not just for you but for all those around you.

The Six-Month Program

A tree as great as a man's embrace springs from a small shoot;
A terrace nine stories high begins with a pile of earth;
A journey of a thousand miles starts under one's feet.

—Lao Tsu

In today's world, time is precious, and free time is rare. We never seem to have the time to invest in our health and self-development, yet we have no qualms about spending countless hours in pursuit of the mighty dollar. Think about those times when you have a headache, the flu, a back ache, whatever. Is it possible to enjoy yourself at those moments, no matter how much money is in your bank account? Why not spend some time, not a lot of time, trying to stay as healthy as possible.

This program presents three options. There is a minimum practice, a short program, and a long program. There will be days when you are just too busy to do your workout. If this is the case, then do the minimum practice, which takes just 5 minutes. A few minutes of daily practice is far more valuable than an hour of practice when you don't have time for it. If you put in a lot of time but miss several days, your progress will be slow, and you will not be optimizing the effectiveness of the exercises. Some teachers believe that if you miss one day it takes three days to get back where you were. Practicing for at least 5 minutes every day guarantees that you will not backslide in your energetic progress. Five minutes daily ensures that every moment of your training is never wasted and that your effort will bear fruit.

The short program requires 25 minutes a day. While 5 minutes a day serves as a healthy minimum, 25 minutes a day is a solid Chi Kung workout. Twenty-five minutes a day is more than enough time not only to maintain, but to regain health and vigor. The short program has two options. Option one stays with the fundamental basics for most of the program. This includes resting the mind, cleansing the body of stress and negative energy, stretching the body, and intensifying the energy of the body. Option two allows you to experience all of the exercises offered in this book while maintaining a constant routine. This option always includes Still Meditation and the Cleansing Exercises but teaches you new exercises too.

The long program requires 30–45 minutes a day. The long program is recommended if you are a martial artist, have aspirations to become an energy healer, if pain relief and health are your priorities, or if you simply enjoy Chi Kung and the benefits it offers. The more you practice, comfort and schedule permitting, the faster your progress and the deeper your experience will be.

You can switch back and forth between the minimum practice, short, and long programs. If your goal is to do the long program, then you will practice for 45 minutes daily, most of the time, sometimes practice for 25 minutes, and only occasionally practice for 5 minutes a day. If you are participating in the short program, you should usually practice for 25 minutes daily, sometimes practice for 5 minutes, and occasionally practice for 45 minutes.

It is not a problem if all you can commit to is the minimum practice of 5 minutes a day. Five minutes can be fantastic if your perseverance and will are directed. Push yourself to practice for 5 minutes a day for 45 days and you will succeed. If you can do this, you will develop consistency. Consistency produces habitual practice. Habitual practice breeds natural practice. Natural practice makes the practice enjoyable. When you enjoy the practice, you will reap the benefits. When you reap the benefits your perseverance and will to practice will strengthen. To activate this cycle it will take 5 minutes a day for 45 days.

THE SUCCESS CYCLE

Desire for Improvement

Reap the Benefits   Perseverance and Will

Enjoyment   Consistency

Natural Practice   Habitual Practice

THE THREE REGULATIONS

There are three basic requirements for developing the energy. They are proper breathing, mind intent, and correct body posture. Without these three prerequisites, energy cultivation is for the most part slow and inefficient.

1. The breathing must be slow, deep, even, and natural. Breathe slowly as this will relax the body, calm the emotions, and settle the mind. Breathe deeply by lowering your respiration to the abdomen area. Feel the diaphragm expand fully in all directions when you inhale, and contract when you exhale. Breathe evenly and let your breathing become subtle. The masters of Chi Kung breathe so evenly that the distinction between inhalation and exhalation is almost indiscernible. Breathe naturally and never force your respiration. Forced breathing is used in some advanced and martial Chi Kung routines, but if you are not familiar with advanced techniques, this can be physically harmful to the body.

2. The mind must be able to visualize, focus, and relax. Energy cultivation is enhanced and catalyzed by utilizing imagination and visualization. The power of your imagination, its clarity, and your acceptance of your visualizations directly influence your ability to cultivate the chi. The mind must be focused but relaxed. If you focus too hard you will create mental tension. If the mind is too relaxed it wanders or you fall asleep. A balance between

focus and relaxation is what you will continually strive for. Staying mentally present and not being too ambitious will allow this balance between focus and relaxation to take place.

3. The body must have correct posture. In the body, energy moves like water through a series of rivers, or "meridians." If the body is posed correctly, the flow of energy throughout the meridian system is optimized. If the body posture is off, the meridians will "crimp," inhibiting chi flow. Also incorrect body alignment causes the muscles to exert too much effort in keeping the skeletal structure erect and balanced. This creates tension in the muscles and restricts chi flow. Having good posture alleviates the work of the muscles so that one is free to relax, and the chi is free to flow.

In all of the exercises in this book you must always maintain proper posture and skeletal alignment to optimize energy flow. Although we show most exercises in a standing position, you can sit as well. You can derive the full energetic benefit in a sitting position if you maintain proper posture and follow the three regulations.

HOW TO STAND

The following is a description of how to stand whenever you perform a Chi Kung movement. The hand positioning will vary depending on the movement.

Stand with the toes pointing forward and the knees slightly bent, the feet a little wider than shoulder-width apart. Your weight should be on the back or heel half of the foot. Never let the knees bend past the toes, and never torque the knees to force the toes in, because over time this may cause damage to the knee.

Roll the hips in and under as if you are sitting on a bar stool. Push out the Gate of Life point, which is located on the lower spine, even with the navel. This is the most important body adjustment you will make. It unites the upper body with the lower body and creates an energetic connection to the ground. Holding this posture will also stimulate the kidney energy, which supports the other organs of the body.

Keep the back straight. Let the shoulders drop and collapse inward, allowing the upper back to spread. This will open the "Spirit Gate," which is located on the spine right behind the sternum. Opening the Spirit Gate is analogous to opening a "spigot" and allowing the energy to flow through.

Tuck the chin in and gently press the crown point of the head up. This adjustment will straighten the back of the neck and open the "Jade Pillow Point," which can be found where the base of the skull and the neck meet. The Jade Pillow Point is another spigot that needs to be opened.

Touch the tongue to the roof of the mouth and at the same time gently close the anal sphincter—this acts as a bridge connecting the main two meridians of the body. Use the same amount of effort closing the anal sphincter as you would shutting your eye.

The combined effect of all these adjustments will be to elongate and stretch the spine, allow the body to relax while standing erect, and encourage smooth energy flow throughout the body.

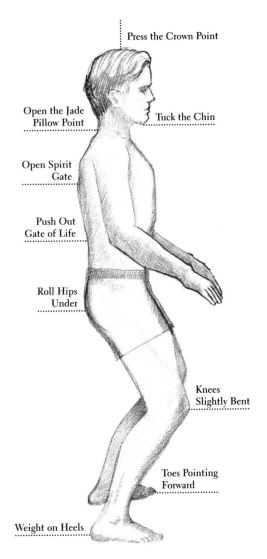

How to Stand.

HOW TO SIT

Sit in a strong, sturdy chair. Scoot forward with the buttocks near the front edge of the chair. The feet are shoulder-width apart and flat on the ground. The knees are bent so that the thighs and lower leg form a 90-degree angle. Push out the Gate of Life point, or lower back. Even in the sitting position, roll the hips in and under. Keep the back straight, and let the shoulders drop and collapse inward, allowing the upper back to spread. Tuck the chin in and press the crown point of the head up, straightening the neck. Touch the tip of the tongue to the roof of the mouth and gently close the anal sphincter.

Month One

Stillness and Movement

The Lotus meditation pose.

In the beginning it is best not to do too much. If you put too much time in initially, then more often than not you will burn yourself out. Your time commitment should build as your interest builds. This is why we do not administer the long program until the third month. If you are healing a specific ailment, then more practice is encouraged.

In the first month you will learn Still Meditation, stretching the back, and loosening and opening the joints of the body. Still Meditation relaxes the mind and relieves mental stress. Stretching the back and keeping the spine supple, what I refer to as "Back Stretches," is central for good physical health. Opening and loosening the joints promotes circulation and also rids the body of physical tension.

There is leeway in the amount of time you spend on each particular exercise because only you can feel what you need. For example, if you have a very stiff back, then spend more time on the back stretches. If you have a mentally stressful life, then spend more time doing Still Meditation. If a particular exercise feels good and is enjoyable, then do more of it. Your body and instincts will guide you to what is needed and what is right for you.

Week One

Minimum Practice	Still Meditation (5 minutes)
Short Program	Still Meditation (5–25 minutes)

Week Two (New: Back Stretches)

Minimum Practice	Option 1: Still Meditation (5 minutes)
	Option 2: Back Stretches (5 minutes)
Short Program	Still Meditation (5–15 minutes)
(15–25 minutes)	**Back Stretches (10–15 minutes)**

Weeks Three and Four (New: Opening the Gates)

Minimum Practice	Option 1: Still Meditation (5 minutes)
	Option 2: Back Stretches (5 minutes)
	Option 3: Opening the Gates (5 minutes)
Short Program	Still Meditation (5–10 minutes)
(20–25 minutes)	Back Stretches (5–10 minutes)
	Opening the Gates (10–15 minutes)

STILL MEDITATION

Movement overcomes cold.
Stillness overcomes heat.
Stillness and tranquillity set things in order in the universe.
— Lao Tsu

It is traditional and highly recommended to begin every workout with Still Meditation. Still Meditation is sometimes referred to as "quiet sitting" or "Wu Chi." It basically means to do nothing. This is not so easy. It is one thing to keep the body still, but another to keep the mind quiet and still. One technique you can use to do this is to count one through ten, over and over. Try not to go to eleven, twelve, and so on. Always return to one. When you inhale, count one, exhale, count two, and so on. This may sound like a silly exercise, but it isn't. The counting will keep you conscious and present and prevent the mind from drifting. The simplicity of the task will allow the mind to relax.

The benefits of Still Meditation are many. Meditation will clear and relax the mind. This allows the body to relax and increases sensitivity. Increased sensitivity enables you to feel the energy. Once you feel the energy, cultivating it becomes much easier. You will also be able to feel where you are tight and tense. This awareness allows you to work out the tension through exercises that will be taught later. When the mind is still, the creativity will come. Our innate genius is always present and available to us, but we cover it up with an array of extraneous thinking. Our minds are like a radio with too many interfering signals coming in. When the interference is decreased the clarity increases. Through meditation you will also become a quiet, objective observer of your own thought processes. This allows you to understand the motivation of your thoughts, emotions, and actions. If something is bothering you but you understand the source, then you can frequently find the folly of your fixation. This lets you release the problem, allowing the mind to relax even more deeply.

In essence Still Meditation is a way to get in touch with your true self. It clears the slate of the illusions, tensions, and worries that accumulate in daily life. It removes the blinding fog that keeps us from experiencing our potential. So important is Still Meditation to our well-being that we begin every workout of our program with it.

There are different postures you may assume in doing Still Meditation. You may either stand, sit, or lie down. The sitting positions are recommended for most people. The lotus sitting position or half-lotus is traditional. The crossing of the legs helps seal the energy and consciousness in the lower abdomen. Bear in mind that you are doing the Still Meditation to clear the thoughts and relax the mind, so if the lotus positions are uncomfortable and distracting, do the sitting chair position instead. The sitting chair position allows you to relax and maintain good posture. If you are unable to sit comfortably, then do the lying down position. It is easy to fall asleep lying down, so only do this position if you have to.

The standing position is good if you are a martial artist or if you want to build strength in your legs. But this position is only recommended if you can still the mind and not let the leg muscles distract your peacefulness. We recommend that you try the sitting postures first and try the standing position later if you feel compelled to.

Lotus Meditation—Sit in a full lotus, half-lotus, or just with the feet crossed. Keep the back straight and the chin pulled in. Feel your entire body relax. Feel tension and tightness leave the body like steam coming out of the pores. Feel your head rest on the vertebrae of the neck. Feel the vertebrae of the neck being supported by the vertebrae of the spine. Now allow the entire spine to relax as it rests upon the pelvic bone in the trunk region. Feel the shoulders relax and drop as this feeling of restfulness extends all the way into the hands and fingertips.

Lotus Meditation—Breathe slowly, smoothly, deeply, and evenly. Pretend there is a balloon in your lower abdominal region. Feel the abdomen expand as you inhale and contract as you exhale. Feel the body relax more deeply with each breath. Begin counting one to ten. When you inhale count one, when you exhale count two, and so on. Let the mind relax. Acknowledge your thoughts and then let them go.

Sitting Chair Meditation (next page)— Sit with the buttocks near the edge of a strong, stable chair. The thighs and lower

legs form a right angle. Keep the lower back pushed out by rolling the hips under. Keep the back straight. Tuck in the chin. Rest the hands on the thighs. Feel your shoulders relax and sink. Feel a wave of relaxation descend from the top of the head down into the shoulders, chest, midsection, arms, and all the way to the fingertips.

Feel this restfulness continue down into the lower abdomen, thighs, calves, feet, and all the way to the toes. With each breath feel your body melt into the chair. Count from one to ten. Inhale and count one, exhale and count two, and so forth. Let any worries drift away. Let the mind unwind.

Standing Meditation (below)—Stand with the feet slightly wider than shoulder width. The hands are out to the sides even with the hips. Roll the hips under the torso. It should feel like you are sitting on a bar stool. The lower back is pushed out. Keep the back

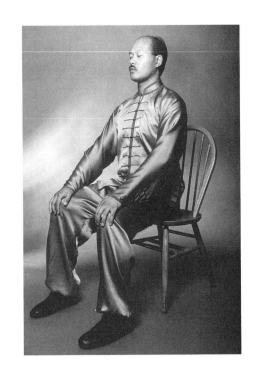

straight and the chin tucked in. Relax the shoulders and let them drop. Feel the weight of your body in the heels of your feet. Feel the weight of the hips over the heels. Feel the vertebrae of the spine stack on top of the tailbone. Feel the head rest on the spine. The muscles should feel like they are hanging from the bones. Breathe deeply and evenly. As you inhale count one, as you exhale count two, and so forth. Let go and drift into a state of conscious relaxation.

Lying Meditation— Lie flat on the ground. The hands are to the sides. Make sure the body is symmetrical and comfortable. Bring your awareness to the entire backside of your body, especially those parts that contact the surface you are lying on. Relax and feel your entire body being supported by the earth. Feel the abdomen expand as you inhale and contract as you exhale. With each breath relax more and more. Now feel your entire front side relaxing. Now imagine the top layer of your body melting all the way through to the bottom layer of your body. Feel the bottom layer of your body melting into the earth. With each breath feel yourself sinking deep into the surface of the earth. Count from one to ten. Inhale and count one, exhale and count two, and so forth. Stay present within your body. Do not fall asleep. Feel the mind let go of anger, fear, worry, and sorrow. Let go of negative emotions and let them drift out of the body.

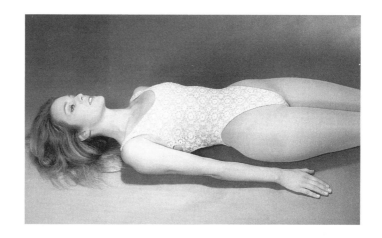

STILL MEDITATION SENSATIONS

You will experience a variety of physical sensations, some pleasurable and some uncomfortable. As time passes, the discomforts will diminish, and the good feelings will increase. The following chart outlines some of the physical sensations you may experience. There are also a variety of mental and emotional sensations that may occur. For instance, your mind may race, and your thoughts may be scattered. The Chinese call this the "Monkey Mind." This is quite common and natural. When this happens, acknowledge the thought, comprehend it, and then release it. Do not try to block the thoughts, just let them happen and do not dwell on them. Some people get fidgety and have a strong aversion toward stillness, while others may breathe very shallowly and quickly, as if they cannot get enough air. Just relax and concentrate on breathing deeper. You may have to limit your time per session, but you can compensate by meditating more frequently.

Aching shoulders	This is normal at first, but make sure your shoulders are relaxed and drooping.
Aching neck	You could be holding mental tension.
Aching knees	Check that your weight is distributed evenly, and make sure that the knees are not bent forward past the toes.
Aching back	Check your posture. Make sure the hips are rolled in and under.
Aching arms	This is normal at first. Try the Swaying Exercise on page 56.
Aching legs	This is normal at first.
Aching feet	This is normal at first.
Headache	Direct your awareness toward your feet. See the "Specific Ailments" section, page 105.
Bloated stomach	Your breathing may be forced. Do the Stomach Massage on page 132.
Sweating	This is normal, a sign that the body is detoxing.
Numbness	This is normal, a sign that chi is flowing.
Tingling	This is normal, a sign that chi is flowing.
Body heat	This is normal, a sign that chi is flowing.
Trembling	This is normal, a sign that the body is detoxing.
Feeling asymmetrical	This is normal, a sign that the body is trying to rebalance itself.
Burping and flatulence	The body is discharging toxins.
Diminishing or no sensations	This is normal. The nature of chi development is that sensations come and go.
Aching old injuries	This is normal, a sign that chi is flowing.

STRETCHING THE BACK

The supple can overcome the stiff.
Under heaven everyone knows this,
Yet no one puts it into practice.

—Lao Tsu

In order for the chi to flow, the mind must be calm, and the body must be relaxed, loose, and free of tightness. Still meditation will calm the mind and relax the body. Stretching will remove tightness and tension, which constrict energy flow. Energy has a difficult time passing through hard, tense muscles. Also tight muscles can cause the skeletal structure to misalign. Misalignment of the body can "pinch off" the rivers of energy that circulate throughout the body. Stretching will relax and nourish the muscles, restoring suppleness and alignment, thereby making it as easy as possible for the energy to flow.

The most important area of the body to keep supple is the back or, more specifically, the spine. It cannot be overemphasized how central the suppleness of the spine is for good health. All of the Eastern athletic arts (Yoga, kung fu, Tai Chi, Chi Kung, and so forth) give special attention and care to the health of the spine. There are many reasons for this. The main pathways of the nervous system run along the spine. Therefore damage to the spine cripples the nervous system. The cerebral spinal fluid, which feeds and nourishes the brain, flows through the spine. The Governing meridian, one of the main energy pathways of the body, also flows through the spine. The Governing meridian connects with the Conceptional meridian to form the Microcosmic Orbit. The Microcosmic

Orbit runs up the back and down the front of the torso and serves as a major passageway for all the rivers of energy. Suppleness of the spine allows the energy to flow smoothly through this major passageway. Just about every movement a person makes involves the spine. Think about how difficult it is to do anything when the back is stiff and sore. The brain may be the commander of the soul, but the spine is the centerpiece of the body.

Oftentimes the biggest obstruction to a healthy back is fear, fear of moving the back. We call it the "traction mentality." Once the back is stiff and sore, people are afraid to move the back for fear of further damaging it. Sometimes these fears are founded, but sometimes they are not, so if you are afraid you have injured your back you should check with your doctor. Instead of dealing

and working with the pain and stiffness, people often deny that a solution is possible and stop trying to heal the back. This way the problem will only worsen. The

Opening the Gates

The back stretching exercises clear the physical constraints that restrict the flow of energy through the Microcosmic Orbit. The Opening the Gates Exercises are stretching exercises that remove the constrictions that inhibit the rivers of energy that flow from the Microcosmic Orbit. These other main rivers flow through the torso and limbs of the body. Their flow of energy will tend to be blocked at or near the joints of the body. These points are called "gates." The work of this section is to open these gates by loosening the main joints of the body—the wrists, elbows, shoulders, neck, waist, knees, and ankles. Promoting flexibility in these areas allows the energy to flow smoothly through the torso and limbs and helps the body move freely and easily.

Shoulder Rotations (30–90 seconds)—Rotate the right arm backward with the palm facing out. The left palm rests by the stomach. As the right hand rotates backward, keep the eyes fixed on the back of the hand. Alternate and circle the left hand backward as the right palm rests by the stomach. Remember to keep the eyes on the back of the hand. This exercise was taught to me by Gene Wong of Vancouver, Canada. When I met Mr. Wong he was a seventy-five-year-old man

who looked like he was fifty, and he had the exuberance of a twenty-five-year-old. He claimed that this exercise was the secret to his good health.

Feel the shoulders, neck, arms, and chest stretch with each rotation. Remember to keep looking at the back of the hand. This will exercise the eyes. The more you turn and look back, the better the stretch. Feel the tension leave the body with each rotation.

Shoulder, Wrist Torque (30–90 seconds)—Stand comfortably with your hands out to your sides at shoulder

height. Turn to the right. Rotate the right palm clockwise as far as you can. Simultaneously rotate the left palm clockwise as far as you can. Feel the waist, shoulders, and wrists stretch and twist. It's as if you are wringing out any tension in the shoulders, arms, and torso.

Return to a neutral position. Relax and inhale. Keep the arms out to the sides at shoulder height.

Turn to the left and exhale. Rotate the left palm counterclockwise as far as you can. Simultaneously rotate the right palm counterclockwise. Relax and feel the muscles, tendons, and ligaments stretch. Alternate between turning to the left and turning to the right. Inhale in the neutral position and exhale in the twisted position.

Elbow, Chest Stretch (30–90 seconds)—Stand with the feet wide apart. The hands are to the side at shoulder height, palms up, as if you are holding a plate in each hand. Rotate the palms back while pushing the chest forward. Feel the elbows and chest stretch. Feel the upper back arching. As you inhale feel the chest expand and open. As you exhale feel the entire body relax.

Now rotate the hands forward and turn the elbows up, causing you to bend forward. The palms should be facing up. Feel the muscles, tendons, and ligaments stretch from the fingertips all the way to the shoulders. Alternate and rotate between elbows up and elbows down. The body alternates from rocking forward to rocking backward.

Waist Rotation (30–90 seconds)—Stand comfortably. Turn to your right as far as you can. The palms face down at waist level, and the fingers point at each other. Feel the stretch in the waist. Look back to your left to stretch the neck. The more you relax, the more you turn.

Switch and turn to the left. Look back to the right. As you twist back breathe deeply, relaxing the waist and lower back. Feel the muscles stretch, allowing the midsection to release and let go.

Knee Rotations (30–90 seconds)—Sit down and clasp your hands underneath your left thigh. Tuck your right foot underneath you. Hold up your left knee with

your arms. Gently rotate the left knee clockwise and counterclockwise. The larger the circle the better. Switch and rotate the right knee. Feel the knee joint warm and loosen.

Ankle Rotations (30–90 seconds)— From a sitting position, the right leg stretches forward. The left ankle rests on the right leg. The left hand grabs the right knee for support. The right hand holds the left foot and rotates the ankle. Rotate both clockwise and counterclockwise. Switch sides and rotate the right ankle with the left leg forward.

SUPPLENESS SENSATIONS

As with any stretching exercises, you may feel sore the next day. Work through the soreness and do not try to make large strides quickly. Try for small gains slowly. Since this routine heavily emphasizes relaxing the back and assumes that most people do not stretch and torque the back, your back will probably get sore. This is okay as long as the soreness is mild and does not limit your movement. (Please check with your doctor if there is any cause for worry.) Approach these exercises as a self–body massage, a method to release stress and tension and a way to become in touch with your body. Notice how animals stretch. Does it look like work, or does it look like pleasure?

Month Two

Emptying and Filling

The Small Orbit Exercise.

In the second month you will learn two basic and essential Chi Kung exercises, the Cleansing Exercises and the Small Orbit Exercise. In month one you increased your sensitivity by clearing the mind with Still Meditation. You also removed physical tightness by stretching and loosening the body. Your mind and body are now prepared to allow the energy to move and circulate. The Cleansing Exercises shake up the body and stimulate the energy while expelling negative and stagnant energy from the body. The Small Orbit Exercise increases the circulation of chi in the main river, or Microcosmic Orbit, and energizes the entire body.

Weeks Five and Six (New: Cleansing Exercises)

Minimum Practice (5 minutes)	Option 1: Still Meditation (5 minutes) Option 2: Back Stretches (5 minutes) Option 3: Opening the Gates (5 minutes) **Option 4: Cleansing Exercises (5 minutes)**
Short Program (20–25 minutes)	Still Meditation (5–10 minutes) Back Stretches (5 minutes) Opening the Gates (5 minutes) **Cleansing Exercises (5 minutes)**

Weeks Seven and Eight (New: Small Orbit Exercise)

Minimum Practice **(5 minutes)**	Option 1: Still Meditation (5 minutes)
	Option 2: Back Stretches (5 minutes)
	Option 3: Opening the Gates (5 minutes)
	Option 4: Cleansing Exercises (5 minutes)
	Option 5: Small Orbit Exercise (5 minutes)
Short Program **(25 minutes)**	Still Meditation (5–10 minutes)
	Back Stretches and Opening the Gates (5–10 minutes)*
	Cleansing Exercises (5 minutes)
	Small Orbit Exercise (5–10 minutes)

* The time needed for stretching may start to decrease. Once the body is loosened and the energy is flowing, tension in the back and joints may disappear. You can then start to pare down the stretching routine to the few exercises that you feel are necessary.

CLEANSING EXERCISES

One gains by losing
And loses by gaining.
—Lao Tsu

By aligning the body, relaxing the muscles, and opening the joints of the body, stretching can open the rivers of the energy. Although the pathways of the energy can be free of kinks and the joints of the body can be open and flexible, the energy itself may still need to be cleansed. The body can hold and accumulate negative energy in a number of ways. Stress, worry, anger, and tension will cause areas of the body to hold negative energy. Physical inactivity or sitting in one position all day will stagnate the energy. The trauma of physical injuries can foster negative, dense energy. Old, past injuries can create and leave stagnant and hard energy even though the injury has healed on a physical level. Repressed emotions and painful memories can also cause the body to hold negative energy.

Negative energy causes chi blockages. The fewer the chi blockages and the cleaner the energy, the more smoothly the energy will flow. The Cleansing Exercises are designed to break up and dispel excess, stagnant negative energy. The stress, tension, trauma, and repressed emotions of the body are literally shaken out. Chi flow is restored by removing instead of adding. These exercises are particularly effective for people with insomnia and for people who sit in front of a computer all day.

Swaying (2 minutes)—Stand comfortably with proper posture. As the hands sway back, exhale. As the hands swing forward, inhale. Relax the shoulders and let the motion gently rock the body. As you exhale and swing back, imagine dark energy being expelled from the body. Feel tightness, tension, and negative emotions being purged from the body. As the hands sway forward, imagine that you are inhaling clean white energy.

As you continue to sway, feel your breathing begin to naturally pace itself with the movement. Allow the muscles to relax more and more. Feel the tension in the base of the neck melt away. Feel the hands tingle and get warm. This is energy collecting in the hands. This exercise is very good for arthritis in the hands.

Swaying–Dropping (2 minutes)—Use the same motion as in the previous exercise. As the hands come forward stand on your toes. As the hands come back drop on your heels. As you land throw the hands back as if slinging water off your hands. The dropping motion will break up stagnant energy in the body. As you

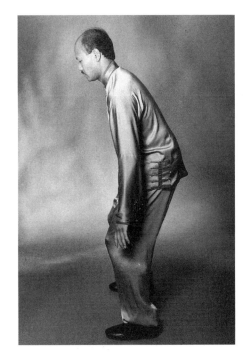

come forward on your toes inhale. As you drop back exhale.

As you sling back imagine dark energy being discharged from the hands. Feel tightness, tension, negative emotions, and stagnant energy being expelled from the body and into the earth. As you continue, feel the body become lighter and lighter.

Shaking (1 minute)—From a standing position shake the hips so that the body trembles. Shake the chest and arms, causing the entire body to tremble. Shake as if your body is shivering. Feel the stagnant energy being broken up

and shaken out of the body. With each repetition the trembling reaches deeper and deeper, allowing the tightness and stagnation to be released outward.

Pulling Down the Heavens (1–3 times)—Circle the arms up over the head and then down in front of the face and torso. As the arms circle up and you inhale, gather energy from the air. As the arms flow down, exhale and imagine cool, heavenly white energy descending into the top of the head, down the face, into the torso, and out through the legs and feet. Feel this heavenly white energy cleaning and cooling the body.

Make it a habit to conclude every Chi Kung session you do with this exercise. This exercise will remove any excess energy that can sometimes linger. Chi Kung can create a great deal of body heat. This exercise will cool you down.

CLEANSING SENSATIONS

The most common occurrence during Chi Kung practice is the generation of a great deal of heat. When chi blockages are broken up and dispersed you will feel warm and even hot energy. You may also perhaps smell odors. When old, stagnant energy leaves the body it sometimes has an odor. Some claim that the smell is like that of an old, mildewy house. You may even experience negative emotions leaving the body. You may feel anger, sadness, fear, or worry for a moment or even for a while, followed by a feeling of lightness, relief, and/or settledness.

*T*HE SMALL ORBIT EXERCISE

With Still Meditation you increase your sensitivity. The Stretching Exercises remove the tension that inhibits the flow of energy through the rivers of energy. The Cleansing Exercises also clear away constraints of chi flow while cleaning the energy. Your body is now prepared to directly intensify the volume and flow of energy. If you try to directly increase chi circulation with the Small Orbit Exercise before preparing the body properly, your progress will not be as fast. If you do not precede this exercise with Cleansing Exercises you may circulate negative energy. Although the Small Orbit Exercise can help cleanse the body, by itself it is not the optimal way to develop the internal energy.

The Small Orbit Exercise activates and stimulates the Microcosmic Orbit. The Microcosmic Orbit serves as a main highway for the meridians of the body. All of the primary meridians flow through the Microcosmic Orbit at some point. There are two main meridians that constitute the Microcosmic Orbit. The "Governing" meridian runs from the perineum up the spine, over the top of the head, down the face, and to the roof of the mouth. The "Conceptional" meridian begins at the tip of the tongue, runs down the throat, descends the front of the body, and connects with the perineum (see diagram). The reason you always place the tip of the tongue on the roof of the mouth and close the anal sphincter is that the Conceptional and Governing meridians connect at these two points. These physical connections serve as energetic bridges for the flow of energy through the Microcosmic Orbit. When the Microcosmic Orbit fills up, it overflows and feeds the other meridians of the body. Various kung fu and Chi Kung styles base their energy development on opening and filling the Microcosmic Orbit because it nourishes the entire body. Imagine the network of meridians of the body as a series of roads through a city. When there are backups traffic can move, but it can only move slowly. Opening the Microcosmic Orbit is like installing a major highway to expedite and alleviate the flow of traffic. It is important to open the Microcosmic Orbit if you want to be an energy healer or martial artist. Opening the Microcosmic Orbit is desirable but not essential for good health, because there are other ways to influence the meridians of the body.

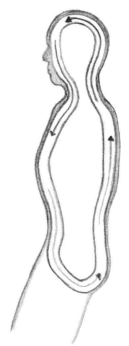

The Microcosmic Orbit.

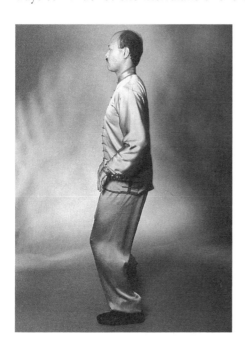

The Small Orbit Exercise (5–10 minutes; this exercise can be done for much longer)—Stand with feet shoulder-width apart. Maintain good posture as you roll the hips under, push out the lower back, pull the chin in, and relax the shoulders. With the palms facing down, raise the hands up the torso. Inhale and imagine

energy ascending from the perineum up the spine to the top of the head. As the hands reach chin height, arc the hands out and let them descend. Exhale and visualize energy descending from the top of the head, down the face, chest, and back to the perineum. Remember to gently close the anal sphincter. This will allow the energy to accumulate in the lower abdomen. Keep the tip of the tongue to the roof of the mouth just behind the teeth.

Inhale as the hands come up, exhale as the hands descend. Coordinate the movement of the hands with the visualization of the energy. Move slowly and feel the energy travel along the Orbit. Gently coax the energy as if you were pulling a silk scarf through a tube. Feel your entire body melt into proper posture.

MICROCOSMIC ORBIT SENSATIONS

While you are trying to open up the Microcosmic Orbit you may feel sensations that mirror your progress. Some people will feel energy starting at the perineum and moving up the sacrum, back, neck, face, then down the chest and stomach, and back to the perineum. This progress is usually slow and gradual and can take several months. The energy may feel like heat, warm air, tingling, numbness, electricity, coldness, or a crawling sensation. Do not let heat or energy accumulate in the head as this will cause headaches. This condition is usually caused by having strong intent guiding the energy up the back but weak intent guiding the energy back down the front. If this happens, imagine you are standing underneath a waterfall. Feel the water washing through you from the top of the head, down the body, and out the feet. You can also do the Pulling Down the Heavens Exercise (page 59) several times; it works well to alleviate this problem.

You may also have strange and intense dreams. Do not let this disturb you. This is usually a good sign that the energy is beginning to flow and that the mind is detoxing itself of negative thoughts.

You may feel nothing but still get a sense of well-being from the exercise. When you practice Chi Kung you are being affected physically, mentally, emotionally, and spiritually. You may be evolving on a spiritual or mental level, but change on the physical level may not be readily apparent. This is very common.

Eventually, the Microcosmic Orbit may open and a new set of sensations may occur. In an open Orbit energy flows freely over its entire length. Like a network of streets that finally has a big highway to keep traffic moving, the energy will flow much more smoothly and strongly throughout the body. When this happens you may see auras, your perception may become very keen, you may feel an internal wind, the saliva may taste sweet, or your body may heat up easily. A multitude of other strange sensations may occur.

Month Three

Building

The Heart Exercise.

In the previous exercises we were affecting the body on a general level. Now we are getting more specific. Month three teaches the Five Element Exercises, which stimulate the energy of the five main organs of the body. These exercises increase circulation along the rivers of energy that flow to the five Yin organs. This is achieved through specific body movements, deep breathing, and the use of the imagination. The Five Element Exercises are very good for maintaining health, but they are even better for regaining health because they affect the functioning of the often mistreated organs. These exercises are similar to Tai Chi movements in that they circulate the chi throughout the entire body and physically keep the body strong and supple. If you practice Tai Chi, these exercises are a good substitute if you do not have the time or space that Tai Chi requires.

Week Nine (New: Water and Wood Exercises)

Minimum Practice (5 minutes)	Option 1: Still Meditation (5 minutes)
	Option 2: Back Stretches and Opening the Gates (5 minutes)
	Option 3: Cleansing Exercises (5 minutes)
	Option 4: Small Orbit Exercise (5 minutes)

Week Nine (New: Water and Wood Exercises) (*cont'd*)

Short Program (25 minutes)	Option 1: Still Meditation (5–10 minutes) Back Stretches and Opening the Gates (5–10 minutes) Cleansing Exercises (5 minutes) Small Orbit Exercise (5–10 minutes) Option 2: Still Meditation (5–10 minutes) Cleansing Exercises (5 minutes) **Water Exercise (5 minutes)** **Wood Exercise (5 minutes)**
Long Program (30–45 minutes)	Still Meditation (5–10 minutes) Back Stretches and Opening the Gates (5–10 minutes) Cleansing Exercises (5 minutes) Small Orbit Exercise (5–10 minutes) **Water Exercise (5 minutes)** **Wood Exercise (5 minutes)**

Week Ten (New: Fire and Earth Exercises)

Minimum Practice **Short Program** **(25–30 minutes)**	(same as above) Option 1: (same as above) Option 2: Still Meditation (5 minutes) Cleansing Exercises (5 minutes) Water Exercise (3 minutes) Wood Exercise (3 minutes) **Fire Exercise (5 minutes)** **Earth Exercise (5 minutes)**
Long Program **(36–45 minutes)**	Still Meditation (5–10 minutes) Back Stretches and Opening the Gates (5–10 minutes) Cleansing Exercises (5 minutes) Small Orbit Exercise (5–10 minutes) Water Exercise (3 minutes) Wood Exercise (3 minutes) **Fire Exercise (5 minutes)** **Earth Exercise (5 minutes)**

Weeks Eleven and Twelve (New: Metal Exercise)

Minimum Practice	(same as above)
Short Program	Option 1: (same as above)
(25–30 minutes)	Option 2: Still Meditation (5 minutes)
	Cleansing Exercises (5 minutes)
	Water Exercise (3 minutes)
	Wood Exercise (3 minutes)
	Fire Exercise (3 minutes)
	Earth Exercise (3 minutes)
	Metal Exercise (3–5 minutes)
Long Program	Still Meditation (5–10 minutes)
(35–45 minutes)	Back Stretches and Opening the Gates (5–10 minutes)
	Cleansing Exercises (5 minutes)
	Small Orbit Exercise (5–10 minutes)
	Water Exercise (3 minutes)
	Wood Exercise (3 minutes)
	Fire Exercise (3 minutes)
	Earth Exercise (3 minutes)
	Metal Exercise (3–5 minutes)

The Five Element Exercises

Taking things lightly results in great difficulty.
Because the sage always confronts difficulties,
He never experiences them.

—Lao Tsu

In the Small Orbit Exercise of month two you intensified the circulation in the main two rivers of energy that constitute the Microcosmic Orbit. We will now increase the energy flow in the smaller primary rivers that flow off the Microcosmic Orbit. These primary rivers flow through the limbs and torso of the body. They also connect with and feed the five main organs of the body, namely the kidneys, liver, heart, spleen, and lungs. These organs are called the five Yin organs. Each organ resides in a pool or lake of energy. Each pool or lake has an energetic quality and is associated with one of the five elements, which exemplifies its essence. For example, the heart is associated with fire, and the heart energy is considered warm and fiery. The kidneys are linked to water, and the kidney energy is cool. The liver is symbolized by wood, and the liver energy is expansive and volatile. The spleen is matched with earth, and the spleen energy is even and stable. The lungs are married with metal, and the lung energy is airy and windlike.

It is important that a balance of energy be maintained in each of these organs. When balance is lost an organ can develop an insufficiency or excess of energy.

According to traditional Chinese medicine, an insufficiency or excess can lead to myriad ailments of varying degrees. The older the problem and the more extreme the imbalance, the worse the ailment (see chart on pages 72–73). Imbalances are usually caused when the river of energy that flows to and from an organ is impeded. When the flow of energy "to" an organ is slowed, an insufficiency of energy occurs. Conversely, when the flow of energy "from" an organ is obstructed, an excess and stagnation of energy arises.

Traditional Chinese medicine holds to the theory that the health of the body is centered on the balance of energy in these five Yin organs or, more precisely, the lakes of energy of these five organs. These lakes of energy influence not only the health of their corresponding organs, but also the health of the complementary Yang organs that are located in or near the Yin organs' lakes of energy. For example, the spleen's complementary Yang organ is the stomach. Both the stomach and the spleen greatly control the digestive process. Each lake of energy also affects the functioning of a corresponding system or systems of the body. For instance, the heart energy, not surprisingly, affects the circulatory system along with the hormonal and endocrine systems. Since the Yin organs have such a strong influence on the entire body, the Chinese use these organs to access the health of the body. With the use of acupuncture, acupressure, herbs, Chi Kung healing, and Chi Kung exercises the Chinese have been quite successful at restoring energy flow to and from an organ, thereby curing an ailment.

The Five Element Exercises are designed to dilate the rivers of energy that flow to and from the Yin organs. The specific movements of the arms and torso help pump energy through the rivers of energy that connect with a specific organ. The vibrancy of the organs is restored and maintained once the energy flow is smooth and even. The movement of each exercise also stretches and warms the region of the body where that particular organ is located. This stretching will gently massage and stimulate the organ. After you have learned all five exercises, do approximately 20–30 repetitions of each movement; each exercise should take about 3 minutes. Maintaining an energetic balance between the five Yin organs, collectively, is also important. Spend equal time with each exercise unless there is a weakness in a particular organ. If this is the case, do twice as many repetitions for the weak organ. You must still do the other exercises because a balance of energy between the organs is important.

Yin Organ	Corresponding Element	Yang Organ	Functions of Organs and Related Systems
Kidney	Water	Bladder	Stores energetic essence Produces marrow and blood Filters nutrients Skeletal, reproductive, and urinary systems
Liver	Wood	Gallbladder	Allows chi to flow freely Stores and filters blood Nervous system Tendons and ligaments
Heart	Fire	Small intestine	Controls blood Regulates circulation Circulatory, hormonal, and endocrine systems Blood vessels Pericardium and Triple Heater*
Spleen	Earth	Pancreas and stomach	Transforms and disperses nutrients Cleanses and stores blood Digestive and lymphatic systems Muscles
Lungs	Metal	Large intestine	Oxygenates blood Disperses chi throughout the body Respiratory and immune systems Skin and hair

* The Triple Heaters relate to three areas of the body which are located in the lower abdomen, midsection, and chest. From an energetic perspective the Triple Heaters regulate the heat of the body and control overall metabolism.

Symptoms of Excess	Symptoms of Insufficiency
	Lethargy
	Ringing in ears
	Hearing problems
	Osteoporosis
	Lack of sexual energy
	Premature ejaculation
	Lower back pain
	Weak, dull hair
	Frequent urination
Tight tendons and ligaments	Weak vision
Muscle spasms and cramps	Weak joints
Hypertension	Chipped and cracked nails
High blood pressure	
Pain in midsection and ribs	
Bloodshot eyes	
Eye pain	
Headaches	
High blood pressure	Low blood pressure
Fast or strong pulse and heartbeat	Poor circulation
Body overheats	Frequently cold
Red face	Pale complexion
Chest pain	Slow or weak pulse and heartbeat
Profuse sweating	
Insomnia	
Excessive hunger	Sluggish digestion
Irregular bowel movement	Bloating
Frequent bowel movement and urination	Weakness in abdominal region
Water retention	Lack of energy
Pain in abdominal region	Tooth decay
Tender gums	Bleeding gums
Presence of phlegm in nose and throat	Lack of muscle tone
Lack of perspiration	Weak respiration
Dry coughs	Sensitive skin
Chest tightness and pain	Oversensitivity to weather change
Coarse, dry skin and hair	Poor circulation
Stiff joints	Sinus congestion
Sinus headaches	Prone to catching colds and flus
	Susceptible to allergies

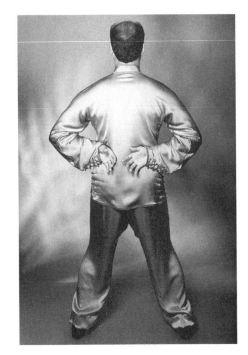

Water Exercise (Kidney)—Stand with the feet wide apart. Roll the hips under and push out the lower back. Place the back of your hands on the lower back, just above the belt, on both kidneys. Turn the hips back and forth to the right and left. Let the hips, not the waist, do the work. Feel the stretch in the pelvis and groin area. Allow heat to accumulate in the kidneys and the back of the hands. As you inhale imagine blue energy coming up from the earth, up the legs and into the kidneys. See the kidneys as beautiful, transparent, deep blue glass jewels. As you exhale imagine dark

energy leaving the kidneys, descending through the legs and down into the ground.

As you turn from side to side, make sure you rotate from the center axis, keeping your spine straight. Gently press up the crown point at the top of your head and imagine that you are suspended by a string.

Water Exercise Part Two—In the same standing position hold the arms like a hoop above the head with the fingers facing each other. Slowly and carefully bend at the waist and rotate the torso. Try to make your rotations as large as possible. Feel the waist, lower back, and sides being stimulated and stretched. Inhale at the top half of the rotation and exhale at the bottom half.

As you inhale feel and see blue energy being drawn up from the earth, up the

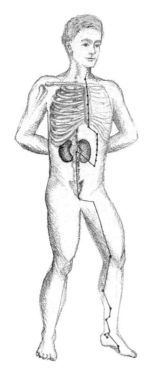

legs and into the kidneys. Visualize the kidneys glowing a vibrant, bright blue. As you exhale feel dark, negative energy flow down the legs. Feel the kidneys being strengthened and cleansed.

This drawing shows the path of the kidney meridian on the left side of the body. Each organ's meridian, or river of energy, runs symmetrically on both sides of the body. As you progress in your training you may feel the energy travel along this pathway.

Wood Exercise (Liver)—Stand with the feet parallel and the toes pointing forward. Tuck in the buttocks and roll the hips under. The hands start out facing down at the level of the hips. Breathe out and push the palms out to shoulder height, as if you were pushing someone away from you. As you inhale, imagine green energy coming up into the legs, into the right side just below the rib cage, and into the liver. Visualize the liver as a translucent emerald green jewel. Feel the liver being energized and nourished. As you exhale, imagine dark, stagnant energy being expelled from the liver and out through the palms. Feel the liver become lighter and more active.

As you push out, gently pull the fingers back, stretching the palms. This will help expel the negative energy out through the hands.

The liver meridian.

The heart meridian.

Fire Exercise (Heart)—Stand comfortably. Pull the hands upward from the waist with the palms facing the body. As the palms reach the solar plexus, push them out to the side and exhale. Stretch the fingers and feel the center of the palms being stimulated. Feel the stretch in the chest, back, and sides. Let the hands drop down, continuing to exhale. Repeat. As the hands come up the torso, breathe in. As the hands press out, breathe out.

As you inhale, imagine red energy coming up the body and into the chest. As you exhale see dark energy push out from the heart, into the arms

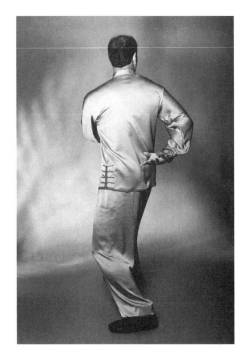

and out the palms. Visualize the heart region glowing a deep ruby red. Feel a warm glow as the heart center is rejuvenated and cleansed.

Earth Exercise (Spleen)—Stand with the legs wide apart. Twist the body to the right. The right arm goes behind the back. The left arm tucks into the midsection. Accentuate the turning motion by twisting the left hand counterclockwise. Exhale as you twist and stretch while feeling the lower abdomen being squeezed like a pump.

Uncoil and return to the neutral position. Inhale gold energy up the legs

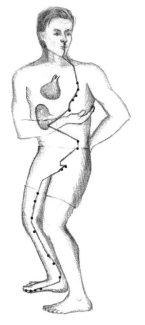

The earth meridian.

and into the spleen. The spleen is located on the left side of the body just under the bottom of the rib cage.

Now twist the body to the left. The left arm goes behind the back. The right arm tucks into the midsection. Rotate the right hand clockwise. Exhale as you turn and compact the body. Breathe and squeeze dark, negative energy out of the spleen. Imagine that the spleen is transforming into a bright gold shape. Feel the spleen being activated and stimulated. Inhale as you twist, exhale as you unwind. Alternate between turning to the left and turning to the right.

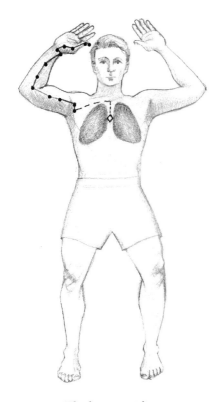

The lung meridian.

Metal Exercise (Lungs)—Stand with the feet wide apart, wrists crossed in front of your chest. Circle the arms up, back behind you and then out to your sides, stretching the chest. As the arms come back in they cross in front of the chest. Stretch the fingers and feel the pull in the palms. Make the circles as large as possible. Feel the back and arms stretch.

Inhale and pull heavenly, white energy into the palms, through the arms, and fill up the lungs. Exhale and let dark, heavy energy flow out and down the body into the earth. See the lungs turn to a bright, pure white. Feel the lungs expand and rejuvenate.

FIVE ELEMENT EXERCISES SENSATIONS

These exercises are designed to stimulate the organs so you may feel them being activated and enlivened. You may feel a gurgling sensation or warmth in a particular organ. In all of these exercises you are encouraged to stretch the tendons by stretching the fingers. This is a technique used by internal martial artists to induce chi flow. As a result you may feel a vibration and heat throughout the torso, limbs, and hands. Sometimes the body can shake and tremble quite strongly. This is good. This is the energy hitting and clearing chi blockages.

Month Four

Purifying

Heart Healing Sound.

THE FIVE ELEMENT PERSONALITY TYPES

It is more important
To see the simplicity,
To realize one's true nature.
—Lao Tsu

Earlier, we mentioned that the energy of each of the five Yin organs has a distinct elemental quality. The Chinese believe that people also have a unique energetic presence. They believe that there are five personality types, and each can be categorized according to the five elements—water, wood, fire, earth, and metal. They believe that we are all a combination of these personalities in varying degrees. It is common to identify strongly with one type, somewhat strongly with another, and possess a few traits of a third. All types have their strengths and weaknesses.

The Chinese believe that if one's personality identifies strongly with a certain element, then the Yin organ associated with that element is more susceptible to an energetic imbalance. For example, a metal type person is more susceptible to lung and respiratory problems than, say, spleen problems. To take this concept even further, the Chinese believe that if somebody's personality is thrown out of balance due to mental stress and frustration, he may develop a physical problem associated with his predominant element and organ. For example, a "wood" person under too much stress may become overbearing, arrogant, and confrontational, and before long he will likely develop an ailment related to the liver energy associated with his wood element. Or, conversely, a medical problem or energetic imbalance in an organ can cause an imbalance in the personality—if a wood person somehow damages the liver or develops a physical problem involving the liver energy, the pain and energy disruption may cause the wood person to become overbearing, arrogant, and confrontational. I cannot overemphasize how helpful it is to understand and heed this relationship between behavior and health. David Nakahara is a classic "earth" person. Earth energy is associated with the spleen. Sure enough, his spleen is sometimes sluggish, and he frequently has minor problems with his digestive system. These problems are usually brought on because he tends to worry a lot, a characteristic typical of an earth person. Nakahara will frequently do Chi Kung exercises involving the spleen and the associated Yang organ, the stomach. This will usually remedy any digestive problem he has. David also finds that when his energy is strong and vibrant he tends not to worry as much. He admits that he is constantly dealing with this delicate balance but that his problems are continually less severe and less frequent. He truly believes that if he could let go of worry he would forever relieve his digestive problems. The personality, the organs, and one's mental and physical health are all related and inseparable. This interconnectedness is the beauty, mystery, and foundation of Chinese philosophy. Everything affects everything, so we must consider and appreciate everything.

There are other important reasons to explore your elemental type. We all have ups and downs in our training. There will be times when you just want to quit. Everyone experiences this. Unfortunately, often people experience these moments of doubt right before a major breakthrough in their training. If you know what element type you are, it may be easier to understand how and why you feel and think the way you do during discouraging moments. Based on this understanding you can work through the self-doubt and frustration to fulfill the reason you are practicing in the first place.

It is also important to understand and embrace your forte. The nature of restoring health and improving yourself is that you deal with your weaknesses. Because of this, it is very easy to forget your strengths. Identifying with an elemental type can help you understand your talents and gifts—we all have so many positive qualities just under the surface, ready to be reaped. We tend to get so caught up in our daily stress and problems that we forget how good we really can be. Being open to the five element personalities will help you remember how much you have going for you.

Understanding your elemental nature will also help you see that your flaws amount to your strengths taken a step or two too far. We have all met people about whom we say, "That guy gets a lot done. He really works hard." About the same person we may also say, "He is unhappy and stressed out. He works too hard." It is important to understand that in searching for the source of our pains, flaws, and weaknesses we are really uncovering, approaching, and embracing our strengths.

THE WATER PERSON

> *The highest good is like water.*
> *Water gives life to the ten thousand things and does not strive.*
> *It flows in places men reject and so is like the Tao.*
>
> —Lao Tsu

The water person is relentless and enduring like the ocean. She has the ability to wait and think herself out of tough situations. She is introspective and blessed with a strong imagination. She is a good listener and observer. She does not get caught up with petty and trivial matters and has the presence of mind to see what is really important. She searches for the truth and has the patience to find it. Her thoughtful and observant nature feeds her natural artistic talents. The water person is independent and self-sufficient, allowing her to be candid and truthful. While the fire person is the center of attention, the water person is usually found in the background.

When water is in motion it stays clean and vibrant. When water stagnates it spoils and is susceptible to contamination. There is danger for the water person in withdrawal and immobilization. The water person is oftentimes a loner. Her introspection can turn into introversion; her disdain for pettiness can cost her her friends; her strong powers of observation can become useless criticism; her search for truth can lead to cynicism. The water person must stay active, positive, and involved and not let her observant and idealistic nature isolate and distance her from other people.

The water person has the ability and courage to look deeply and truthfully at herself. This is 90 percent of the battle. The more honest you are with yourself, the deeper you can look inward, and the more you will let go of negativity. Letting go of negativity will directly enhance energy flow, which will make the body healthier. This desire for truth makes Chi Kung training very powerful and successful for the water person. The water person also enjoys solitude, which allows her to be comfortable with meditation. Like a flowing river, the water person's movements are smooth and fluid and conducive to chi flow. The main pitfall in the water person's training comes when she thinks about it too much instead of just doing it.

THE WOOD PERSON

Thus an army without flexibility never wins a battle.
A tree that is unbending is easily broken.
The hard and strong will fall.
The soft and weak will overcome.

—Lao Tsu

The wood person is strong, bold, and prominent like a great redwood. He is motivated, ambitious, and independent. The wood person is hardworking, decisive, and competitive. He enjoys adventure and challenge and handles adversity very well. He functions well in situations others find overwhelming. His talent for dealing with challenges is such that he sometimes enjoys the chase more than the prize. If you need to get the job done or take the bull by the horns, you need to call upon the wood aspect of your personality. The wood person makes a good leader.

When a wood person is out of balance he becomes inflexible and rigid like a dry piece of wood. Frustration can make him impatient, arrogant, intolerant, and tyrannical. When he gets stopped or slowed down he tends to try harder but often without a smarter approach. When he needs to back off he tends to go forward. His determination can become obsession; his boldness can change to carelessness; his confidence can be repulsive; his competitiveness can create adversaries; he can abuse his power; he tends to pen up and hold in his energy and emotions; he needs to learn to relax, wait, release, and retreat.

In Chi Kung training the wood person is motivated, committed, and has high expectations. He is definitely willing to work. Physically, he moves with power and has good form and posture. The wood person tends to get stiff, so he needs to stay flexible through stretching. He can be too competitive in his training and compare his progress to that of others. This is a major mistake because someone else's progress is totally irrelevant to one's own. Instead of going deeper and further, he can get bored with the training if he feels like he has accomplished his initial goals. He sometimes tries to "force" the energy to flow instead of "letting" the chi flow.

THE FIRE PERSON

> *He who is attached to things will suffer much.*
> *He who saves will suffer heavy loss.*
> *A contented man is never disappointed.*
> *He who knows when to stop does not find himself in trouble.*
> *He will forever be safe.*
>
> —Lao Tsu

The fire person is radiant like a torch. She is vibrant, expressive, alert, and imaginative. The fire person is an excellent communicator and speaker. She is humorous and entertaining and likes to take center stage. Fire people are engaging and can capture the imagination of all present. She is endowed with a passion for life and has a warmth and tenderness that endears her to people. She knows how to enjoy the fruits of her labor and is motivated by sensuality. While the wood person likes the chase, the fire person enjoys the prize. While the wood person makes a good administrator and manager, the fire person is the spark that ignites the action.

A fire can easily burn too hot or be squelched out quickly. Likewise, the fire person is susceptible to extreme mood swings, and her energy can come and go. While her energy can enliven, because she puts out so much, it can also be consuming. In other words, she can burn herself out and also tire those around her. Likewise the fire person's enthusiasm can be difficult to check and can get out of control. Her charm and radiance can be used to seduce and manipulate; her imagination can lead to disillusion; her sensuality can become hedonistic. She needs to understand and control the great power and influence she has on other people.

The fire person approaches her training with enthusiasm and excitement. She is often gifted with a natural talent for energy practice. Her strong imagination allows her to develop the energy quickly. She learns fast because she is alert and attentive. She moves with grace and coordination. Physically and energetically, the fire person is susceptible to overheating. This heat needs to be quelled with the Cleansing Exercises (page 55) and cooled with Pulling Down the Heavens (page 59). The Heavenly Energy Meditation, which is taught later (on page 157), will also cool a fire person's energy. When the fire person hits a plateau in her training, which is inevitable, she tends to get discouraged and bored. She sometimes gets too dependent on the stimuli that energy training has to offer. When these sensations disappear, she perceives this as halting progress, which is a mistake. Her early success is usually the source of her undoing as it can inflate her expectations.

THE EARTH PERSON

In caring for others and serving heaven,
There is nothing like using restraint.
Restraint begins with giving up one's own ideas.
This depends on Virtue gathered in the past.
If there is a good store of Virtue, then nothing is impossible.
If nothing is impossible, then there are no limits.
If a man knows no limits, then he is fit to be a ruler.
The mother principle of ruling holds good for a long time.
This is called having deep roots and a firm foundation,
The Tao of long life and eternal vision.

—Lao Tsu

The earth person is stable like a mountain. He is laid-back, centered, and even keeled. Family, home, and comfort is what is important to the earth person. He is willing to do whatever is necessary to keep things in harmony. The earth person is loyal and faithful. He makes a good friend and a trusted liaison. His supportive, nurturing, and accommodating nature keeps him in the middle of the action. The fire person may be the center of attention, but the earth person is the glue that binds people together. Of the five element personalities, the earth person is the most naturally balanced. In fact, when the five elements are listed they are sometimes configured in a ring; the earth element is oftentimes placed in the middle, representing the stabilizing center.

The earth can become oversaturated, heavy, and muddy. The trap of the earth person is stagnancy and sluggishness. His stability can render him immobile; his desire to nurture and support can become suffocating and fawning; his considerate and sympathetic nature can foster worry and distress; his need for comfort can cause him to stockpile and horde; his ability to negotiate, referee, and compromise can turn into manipulation and control.

The earth person approaches his training with steadiness and practicality. He is good at integrating his practice smoothly into his daily routine. His patience and consistency make him a good candidate to do very well with Chi Kung training. The earth person moves with strength and rootedness. His natural strength in the legs enables him to stand for long periods of time, allowing the energy to store and build. It is easy for the earth person to understand that great energy and power can be extracted from stillness. The earth person must avoid letting the training become monotonous and stale. The excitement of Chi Kung comes from feeling the internal energy and experiencing better health. However, there are times when meditation and Chi Kung can be too physically static and repetitive. The earth person, especially, needs to keep the training fresh and varied. This can be accomplished by changing his routine, practicing in different settings, and even by doing other forms of exercise. Anything that involves movement and change is good for the earth person when he feels like he is stagnating.

THE METAL PERSON

> *The sage is sharp but not cutting,*
> *Pointed but not piercing,*
> *Straightforward but not unrestrained,*
> *Brilliant but not blinding.*
> —Lao Tsu

The metal person proceeds with the precision and definition of a fine blade. Metal represents transformation, distillation, refinement, and sharpness. The metal person is good at cutting through what is unimportant and finding the logic and principle of the matter. She is adept at refining and improving the way things are done. She strives for perfection in herself and others. The metal person will follow principle instead of giving in to selfish needs. She believes in morality and honor, and because of this, she is trusted. The metal person is organized, methodical, and logical. Although the wood person would make a better leader, the metal person makes an excellent planner.

A blade forged from a fine piece of metal has an element of flexibility. A less refined piece of metal is brittle and inflexible. The metal person has to be wary of becoming rigid and close minded. Her methodical and exact way of approaching things can become ritualistic and dogmatic; her morality can turn into self-righteousness; her desire for self-perfection can lead to disappointment and cause her to tighten up; her desire for perfection in others can lead to disillusionment and the inclination to punish and exert control.

The metal person approaches her training systematically and methodically. Her striving for precision and desire for perfection cause her to continually adjust and refine her movements. This allows her to feel and understand how body movement and posture affect chi flow. The metal person must not try too hard to analyze and perfect, because this approach can lead to frustration if taken too far. The metal person must remember that in Chi Kung relaxation is more important than precision. The metal person has an ability to recognize and understand the principles and simplicity of how and why things are done; this is invaluable because the base principles are where the benefits of Chi Kung are derived. It is common to get caught up in the style and tradition of one's teacher, but then one often fails to see the simplicity and reason of a movement. For example, many people will believe an exercise is good because their teacher taught it to them. They may also believe a move is no good because their teacher didn't teach it to them. What is important is to understand the reasons and principles that make an exercise functional. The metal person is good at doing just this.

Week Thirteen (New: Kidney and Liver Sounds)

Minimum Practice **(5 minutes)**	Option 1: Still Meditation (5 minutes) Option 2: Back Stretches and Opening the Gates (5 minutes) Option 3: Cleansing Exercises (5 minutes) Option 4: Small Orbit Exercise (5 minutes)
Short Program **(25 minutes)**	Option 1: Still Meditation (5–10 minutes) Back Stretches and Opening the Gates (5–10 minutes) Cleansing Exercises (5 minutes) Small Orbit Exercise (5–10 minutes) Option 2: Still Meditation (5–10 minutes) Cleansing Exercises (5 minutes) Five Element Exercises (5–10 minutes) **Kidney Sound (2.5 minutes)** **Liver Sound (2.5 minutes)**
Long Program **(30–45 minutes)**	Still Meditation (5–10 minutes) Back Stretches and Opening the Gates (5–10 minutes) Cleansing Exercises (5 minutes) Small Orbit Exercise (5–10 minutes) Five Element Exercises (5–10 minutes) **Kidney Sound (2.5 minutes)** **Liver Sound (2.5 minutes)**

Week Fourteen (New: Heart and Spleen Sounds)

Minimum Practice	(same as above)
Short Program **(25 minutes)**	Option 1: (same as above) Option 2: Still Meditation (5–10 minutes) Cleansing Exercises (5 minutes) Five Element Exercises (5–10 minutes) **Heart Sound (2.5 minutes)** **Spleen Sound (2.5 minutes)**
Long Program **(30–45 minutes)**	Still Meditation (5–10 minutes) Back Stretches and Opening the Gates (5–10 minutes) Cleansing Exercises (5 minutes) Small Orbit Exercise (5–10 minutes) Five Element Exercises (5–10 minutes)

Week Fourteen (New: Heart and Spleen Sounds) (*cont'd*)

Heart Sound (2.5 minutes)
Spleen Sound (2.5 minutes)

Week Fifteen (New: Lung and Triple Heater Sounds)

Minimum Practice	(same as above)
Short Program **(25 minutes)**	Option 1: (same as above)
	Option 2: Still Meditation (5–10 minutes)
	Cleansing Exercises (5 minutes)
	Five Element Exercises (5–10 minutes)
	Lung Sound (2.5 minutes)
	Triple Heater Sound (2.5 minutes)
Long Program **(30–45 minutes)**	Still Meditation (5–10 minutes)
	Back Stretches and Opening the Gates (5–10 minutes)
	Cleansing Exercises (5 minutes)
	Small Orbit Exercise (5–10 minutes)
	Five Element Exercises (5–10 minutes)
	Lung Sound (2.5 minutes)
	Triple Heater Sound (2.5 minutes)

Week Sixteen (Review of All Six Healing Sounds)

Minimum Practice	(same as above)
Short Program **(25 minutes)**	Option 1: (same as above)
	Option 2: Still Meditation (5–10 minutes)
	Cleansing Exercises (5 minutes)
	Five Element Exercises (5–10 minutes)
	All Six Healing Sounds (5 minutes)
Long Program **(30–45 minutes)**	Still Meditation (5–10 minutes)
	Back Stretches and Opening the Gates (5–10 minutes)
	Cleansing Exercises (5 minutes)
	Small Orbit Exercise (5–10 minutes)
	Five Element Exercises (5–10 minutes)
	All Six Healing Sounds (5 minutes)

The Healing Sounds

A brave and passionate man will kill or be killed.
A brave and calm man will always preserve life.
Of these two which is good and which is harmful?
Some things are not favored by heaven. Who knows why?
Even the sage is unsure of this.

—Lao Tsu

In the previous month you learned how to increase chi circulation to and from the five Yin organs of the body. In month four we will learn how to cleanse the Yin organs of negative energy by using the Healing Sounds. The Healing Sounds vibrate the organs and the pools of energy surrounding the organs, causing stagnant energy to dislodge and disseminate. Unlike the Five Elements Exercises, these exercises should not be done all the time. Yet, if performed when needed, they can be so valuable and effective that we feel it is worth spending a month learning and practicing them.

According to traditional Chinese medicine a person's health can be threatened environmentally or internally. Environmental factors are excessive heat, cold, wind, dampness, dryness, bacteria, viruses, and so forth. Invasion by any of these agents can disrupt and weaken a person's chi, thereby causing illness and disease.

Internally, a person can develop an illness through "stuffing" and accumulating negative emotions. Understand that thoughts and emotions are just energy. Have you ever entered a room full of anger, sadness, joy, or agitation and then begun to experience those same feelings? You were merely feeling the emotional energy of the people in the room as it flowed into your body. We are taught to suppress our feelings and emotions for the sake of politeness, dignity, productivity, and survival. If this suppression is taken too far and we hold back and choke our emotions, the energy of the emotions will remain inside the body. If the emotional energy continues to linger, it will condense, coagulate, and harden to form energy blockages. These blockages restrict energy flow, which can then cause illness. Think of those times when you held in your emotions and did not express yourself. Do you remember how stressful, physically agitating, and draining it is to do this? Do you remember how relaxing and how good it feels when you finally express yourself? We do this to ourselves in small degrees constantly.

We also accumulate chi blockages from past traumatic memory. We all have experiences in our past and our childhoods that are so physically and emotionally painful that we can barely recall them if at all. Yet the event will stay in our long-term memory. The Chinese believe that the tissues of the body also have memory. They believe that past traumatic events take on an energetic form and lodge in the tissues. Have you ever felt the pain of an old, past injury long after you have physically healed? Have you ever noticed how your body reacts when remembering an emotionally powerful event? As long as the energy of the event remains in the body, the feelings attached to the event will also remain. Over time this old energy will condense and form an energy blockage. In the short term, the tissues surrounding the blocked area will be tense, receive less blood circulation, be much more susceptible to injury, and/or be overly sensitive to touch. In the long term, according to tradition, this may lead to a tumor or another type of ailment.

Everything you have learned thus far has contributed in some way to clearing and releasing the blockages created by stuffed emotions and past traumatic memory. Still Meditation allows you to become an outside observer of your thoughts and emotions. This objective perspective encourages you to let go of emotion that is pent up and frozen by petty thoughts. The back and joint stretching exercises relax the tissues of the body. Since the energetic blockages are lodged in the tissues, relaxing them allows the hard energy to soften and melt out of the body. The Cleansing Exercises will loosen, break up, and shake out some of these blockages. The Small Orbit and Five Element Exercises will also help remove the blockages. Intensifying the circulation of the energy will dislodge these blockages the way a river's water washes debris from its banks. All these Chi Kung exercises are important but the Healing Sounds are the most direct way to purge the blockages created by the emotions and memory.

Energy blockages created by emotions tend to cluster and connect with the five Yin organs. Interestingly, certain types of emotional energy will attach to specific organs. Fear clings to the kidneys, anger to the liver, overexcitement and anxiety grip the heart, worry lies in the spleen, and grief in the lungs. The Healing Sounds were devised to cleanse the negative emotional energy from the organs and reestablish their energetic vitality. By directing one's awareness and making the appropriate sound, the organ is vibrated, thereby shaking loose the extraneous chi. Cleansing emotional pain through the voice has been around for a long time. It is believed that singing originated not for entertainment but as a way to "cleanse the soul." Singing releases and expresses emotion and vibrates the lower torso where most of the organs are located. The Healing Sounds are just a more systematic, distilled, and specific way to purge emotional energy. Once you have learned all six sounds, do 8–10 exhalations for each organ. (The Triple Heater Healing Sound is the sixth sound. The Triple Heater is an organ system unique to Eastern medicine and is associated with the metabolism. It consists of three heaters, one located in the chest, another in the abdomen, and the third in the lower intestine.)

An organ that needs clearing will tend to cause each exhalation to be short. Try to extend each exhalation for as long as possible. As you exhale the sound, lower the tone of your voice. This helps release the negative energy. With the Triple Heater Healing Sound only, allow the tone to rise as you exhale. When you are feeling distraught by a certain negative emotion, the Healing Sounds can offer relief and comfort.

Kidney Healing Sound—Sit in a chair and bend forward. Feel the stretch in the lower back. Place the right thumb in the left palm. Place your consciousness on the kidneys.

Get in touch with what causes you fear. Go deep in your mind and body and find the root of your fears. Feel any sensations that may come up. These sensations are merely emotions in an energetic state connected to the kidneys. Make the sound "fffuuu . . ." Feel this fear energy release with the vibration. As you exhale imagine dark, stagnant energy leaving the kidneys. Feel the fear leave the body, making you lighter, gentler, and more rejuvenated.

Liver Healing Sound—Place the back of the left hand on the right portion of the lower back just below the rib cage. This is where the liver is located. Extend the right arm up with the palm facing up. Lean to the left, stretching the right side. Place your consciousness on the liver. Get in touch with what causes you anger. Go deep inside yourself and follow the roots of your anger. Feel any sensations that may arise. These sensations are merely emotions in an energetic state connected to the liver. Make the sound "shhhuuu . . ." Feel dark, hot energy release with the reverberation. Feel the liver being cleansed and rejuvenated. As you exhale let anger, impatience, hate, and aggression leave the body. Feel yourself become stronger and more focused.

Heart Healing Sound—Interlock the fingers and press the palms of the hands up above the head. Direct your mind to the heart region in middle of the chest. Get in touch with what causes you uneasiness and overexcitement. Exhale the sound "hhhaaa . . ." Feel the resonance in the heart region. Feel the chest region and upper back relax. Feel the hot, stagnant energy leave the chest. Let agitation and nervousness leave the body. Lower the sound and feel the vibration go deep into the chest. Feel the consciousness become clearer and sense warmth and joy radiating from the body.

Spleen Healing Sound—Put the back of the right hand on the lower left side of the back just below the rib cage. This is where the spleen is located. Extend the left arm up with the palm facing up. Lean to the right, stretching the left side. Direct your awareness to the spleen. Get in touch with what causes you worry and anxiety. Go deep inside your conciousness and trace the source of your worries. Be sensitive to how this makes you feel. Understand that these feelings are just energy associated with the spleen. Make the sound "hhhuuu . . ." Feel and guide the reverberation of the sound down into the spleen. With each exhalation let worry and doubt leave the body. Feel the old, stagnant, heavy energy being released from the spleen. Feel how this cleansing makes you carefree and settled.

Lung Healing Sound—Make sure you have a sturdy chair for the lung healing sound. Lean back and spread out your arms. Feel the stretch in the chest. Place your mind on the lungs. Get in touch with what makes you feel sadness and grief. Allow yourself to go deep inside to trace the seeds of this sorrow. Make the sound

"ssss . . ." Feel the resonance in the chest and lungs. With each exhalation let the entire chest and upper back relax. Feel the lungs expand and contract. Allow sadness and sorrow to leave the lungs as you exhale this sound. Feel the dark, heavy energy leave the lungs. Allow the resonation to become finer and deeper. Feel the spirit become more positive and optimistic.

Triple Heater Healing Sound— Lie flat on your back with your arms to your sides. Exhale the sound "ssseee . . ." Feel the vibration travel from the throat, through the chest, to the midsection, into the abdominal region, and ending at the perineum. On the next exhalation guide the sound from the perineum up the center of the body, ending at the throat. Alternate the direction of the vibration with each exhalation. Experience the vibration like a wave moving up and down the body. Feel tightness, tension, stagnant energy, and negative emotion release as the vibration rolls through the body. Feel a warm glow inside your body and sense an overall increase of energy and well being.

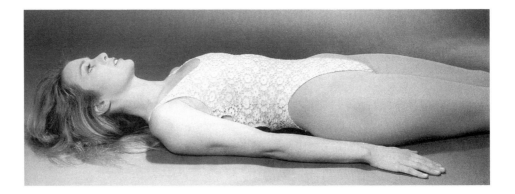

HEALING SOUNDS SENSATIONS

These exercises are designed to cleanse and shake up the five Yin organs. You may actually feel your insides vibrate. Sometimes a dull pain or soreness in an organ may occur. If the soreness is sharp or persists, consult your physician, but a slight pain is usually a good sign. Later you may feel a vibrancy in the organ or the region where the organ is located. You may also notice your stomach or another organ "gurgling." This too is a good sign.

With the Healing Sounds Exercises you are releasing negative emotions that are energetically attached and associated with particular organs. You may experience the emotion as it leaves the body. It is also common to feel nauseous and experience flulike symptoms, headaches, irritability, extreme tiredness, and moodiness. Believe it or not, these are positive signs. If this does happen, it is recommended that you follow the Healing Sounds with the Cleansing Exercises. The Healing Sounds scrub the negative emotions from the organs, and the Cleansing Exercises rinse them away.

You are detoxing emotionally, which is good and desired, but the process can be very uncomfortable, even downright painful. This is when some people stop doing Chi Kung, right at the brink of great progress. Just remember that the discomfort will pass and that the road to real self-development is sometimes rocky.

Specific Ailments

The Stomach Massage.

There is no greater catastrophe than underestimating the enemy.
By underestimating the enemy, I almost lose what I value.

—Lao Tsu

You are at this point in the book either because you have an ailment and need immediate relief or because you have just finished month four of the program. There are a variety of reasons this section is placed so late in the program. There are many aches, pains, and ailments that will be alleviated and disappear when you do the beginning, basic Chi Kung exercises. Many times people will have a variety of problems, and it can be difficult to discern and recognize the main problem until the lesser problems fade away. Of course there are problems that are more acute, defined, and need immediate attention. If this is the case with you, then do the recommended exercises for your particular ailment but partake of the entire program as well. You should spend 10–20 minutes on the exercises that alleviate your problem and participate in the *short* program as well.

As your energy cleanses and increases during the course of this program, you will be more sensitive to factors that affect your health. If you eat the wrong foods, take in drugs, drink too much alcohol, or abuse yourself in any way, your body will respond more strongly than in the past. It's as if your standard for health rises, and your body has become spoiled. You may feel specific problems more readily, but your response to the exercises that solve the problems will likewise be more positive and therapeutic. Do not think of this as sideways progression—that you are only trading gifts for problems. Think of this as achieving deeper and more profound levels of health and vitality.

Self-healing is the oldest, safest, and most natural form of healing, yet in Western society it is usually the last alternative. In China self-healing is the first option. This chapter will not only give you specific methods to deal with distinct problems, but it will also offer insight into the symptoms. This is important because catching the problem early is your best and most effective defense. Body awareness, sensitivity, being in touch with your emotions and mental clarity all make early diagnosis possible. That is why you should try the entire program, because each of these abilities is developed in the first four months.

The ancients believed that all things in the universe are merely energy vibrating at different frequencies. A solid object is energy vibrating at a low frequency, whereas fire is energy vibrating at a high frequency. Because everything is just energy, everything influences everything. Sound, time, location, emotions, heavenly bodies, thoughts, color, light, temperature, weather—all these affect the human body. The ancients also found that the interrelationship between energies and the body is consistent and predictable. They devised a template that represented the cyclic and interdependent relationships of energy. They found that the elements water, wood, fire, earth, and metal exemplified the quality of each type of energy. They also found that all things could be classified according to a particular element, including the functioning of the body.

Over thousands of years, through careful observation and documentation, the ancients were able to draw specific correlations between seemingly diverse physical, mental, and emotional characteristics and the health of the body. For instance, salty saliva, a fearful nature, difficulty hearing, a sore lower back, an aversion to cold, dark circles underneath the eyes, an overly philosophical mentality are all signs of kidney energy out of balance. These findings are founded on an accumulation of experience rather than on scientific testing. For thousands of years traditional Chinese medicine, including acupuncture and acupressure, has successfully utilized these correlations or signals for diagnosis.

As mentioned earlier, the five Yin organs, namely the kidneys, liver, heart, spleen, and lungs, are the hubs of a healthily functioning body. The energy of these organs influences the different systems of the body. Consequently most ailments can be associated with an imbalance of energy in one of these organs.

Hence, if you balance and strengthen the energy of an organ, you can resolve myriad problems associated with that organ. If the energy of one of the five Yin organs is out of balance, then there is either an excess or an insufficiency of energy. We classify the ailments and solutions into three categories: excess, insufficient, and general. If the ailment can be caused by either an excess or an insufficiency, then the ailment is listed in the general column. If a solution can solve an excess or an insufficiency problem, then it is listed as a general solution. As certain ailments can be caused by imbalances in various organs, these ailments are listed under multiple organs. For instance, insomnia can be caused by an energy imbalance in the kidneys, heart, or liver. You must experiment at times to find the appropriate solution. Bear in mind that if you have to try more than one solution you will not have hurt yourself by doing the other exercises—in fact, you will get some energetic benefit, regardless. This is all we can do in this book without the benefit of one-on-one diagnosis, and since this book is not meant to replace a doctor but to supplement his or her treatment, all we wish to do is involve you in the healing process.

KIDNEY ENERGY
IMBALANCES AND SOLUTIONS

In traditional kung fu training the first exercise that is taught is the low Horse Stance. This is because the Horse Stance is a fast and powerful way to restore energy in the kidneys. The kidneys are like a battery that supports the other Yin organs of the body. It is also believed that the kidneys hold our "life-force energy," our original essence, energy inherited at the time of conception. We are born with a finite amount of this energy, and the more we can conserve this life force energy the longer and more healthy our lives may be. If we can continually restore energy in the kidneys we will use less of the original essence we were born with and more of the energy we can create using Chi Kung. If the kidney energy is strong, the entire body will be strong and vital. The kung fu masters, experts in physical development and human power, understood this.

In Western society low kidney energy is extremely common. Since the body demands so much of the kidneys, low kidney energy is common in any society. However, our Western lifestyle is particularly prone to draining energy from the kidneys. Long hours, lack of sleep, too much coffee, too much sex, and sitting all day are all habits common to our highly pressurized society—and all these habits will deplete the kidney energy. The typical scenario for a kidney energy deficient person is thinking too much, working too long, and being under pressure to make a living. This could cause her to lose sleep at night, and since rest is what most helps the kidneys naturally rejuvenate, if they are denied it they will weaken. The person will wake up tired; coffee is the way to perk up, but the caffeine in the coffee drains some of her energy. Her job requires sitting at a desk all day. The kidneys are located in the lower back; sitting all day will tighten and weaken the lower back. A weak lower back drains the kidneys and vice versa—weak kidneys lead to lower back pain. As fear is the emotion associated with the kidneys, the person will likely become fearful for her position at work and insecure about her self-worth. She also may become afraid to move and exercise her lower back. At night, the coffee, the soreness of the back, and the fear for her job and future will make her sleep restless. This is a cycle that easily perpetuates itself. Other problems associated with low kidney energy may develop. At first, the person may simply always feel rundown and tired. She may then become overly sensitive to cold weather and always feel cold. Dark circles may form underneath the eyes, and as the ears are associated with the kidneys, the hearing may be slightly impaired. Sexual energy also is fueled by the kidneys, so sexual vitality may lessen. The bladder is the Yang organ that complements the kidneys, so frequent urination may become necessary. The skeletal system is nourished by the kidney energy, so the bones and joints will weaken. Any or all of these things may happen if you have weak kidney energy.

Have no fear, for the solutions are simple. Get more rest and you will have fought half the battle. Stretch and strengthen the back. Drink herbal tea instead of coffee, or at least drink decaffeinated coffee.

The solutions for the energy imbalances in all five Yin organs are divided into three sections: excess, insufficient, and general. Read the symptoms chart and decide whether you have an excess or lack of energy. If you are not sure, then attempt only the general solutions. With the kidney we concentrate on the lack of energy because, in our experience, this is the problem ninety-nine percent of the time (with other organs the problem may be an insufficiency, excess, or both). Follow the menus and try to do 5–10 minutes of the general solutions and 5–10 minutes of either the insufficiency or excess solutions. Your total time spent on an ailment should be at least 10–20 minutes. If your problem is very uncomfortable, then you can always do more.

KIDNEY ENERGY IMBALANCES

Insufficient Kidney Energy	General Kidney Ailments	Excess Kidney Energy
Lethargy	Fearful nature	
Low sex drive and impotency		
Lower back pain		
Frequent urination		
Knee weakness		
Osteoporosis		
Hearing loss		
Ringing in ears		
Hair loss		
Weak, dull hair		
Prostate problems		
Hormonal imbalance		

SOLUTIONS FOR INSUFFICIENT KIDNEY ENERGY

1. **Gate of Life Prone Position (page 128)**. This is a very gentle exercise, as you are only lying down on your hands. This is a good way to warm up, and it is particularly good if you have lower back pain and stiffness or lethargy.
2. **Kidney Massage (page 128)**. This exercise is quite soothing and gentle. This will warm and stimulate the kidneys. This exercise is also very good for lethargy, lower back pain, and increasing sex drive and potency. This is also a good warm-up and can be done anytime.
3. **Beating and Drumming the Chi (page 129)**. This exercise works very well in conjunction with the Small Orbit Exercise. You will find that this exercise is more effective if you have completed at least month two of the program. This exercise will increase sex drive and potency and maintain health of the prostate.
4. **Bubbling Spring Point (page 136)**. Exercising this point is good for toning the kidney energy, increasing overall energy, and combating fatigue.

5. **Three Yin Crossing Point (page 137).** This point will tone the kidney energy and help with lethargy. It will also promote normal urination and can stop ringing in the ears.

SOLUTIONS FOR GENERAL KIDNEY AILMENTS

1. **Kidney Healing Sound (page 99).** This is particularly good if you believe your problems have to do with fear or other negative emotions, especially if they are stress related.
2. **Water Exercise (page 74).** This exercise should be part of your daily routine. It is very good for building and maintaining overall energy and vitality in the kidneys.
3. **Horse Stance (page 129).** This is an excellent and intense exercise. You need determination and will to do this, but it is the fastest way to restore energy in the kidneys. This exercise will build up strength in the legs.
4. **Holding the Ball (page 149).** This exercise allows you to concentrate and accumulate energy in the lower energy center or lower abdomen. This exercise works best if you have completed month five of the program, but it is a very effective way to balance the energy regardless.

LIVER ENERGY IMBALANCES AND SOLUTIONS

Each of the five Yin organs has a specific energy function. The liver has the responsibility of directing energy throughout the whole body. In traditional Chinese medicine the liver is referred to as the "commander" of the chi. This is fitting because the wood person often has the personality of a leader. The problems of the liver, however, are often caused when a person behaves like a leader out of control.

In the United States qualities such as aggressiveness, toughness, fierceness, loudness, and competitiveness are rewarded. In Eastern culture these qualities are neither good nor bad. What is important is that these traits be appropriate for the situation and that they be balanced with softness. Problems with the liver energy usually occur when a person becomes overly aggressive, too strong, and lets anger overtake his reason. When anger becomes the fuel that drives production, the liver energy will become overactive and volatile. In our society kidney energy is almost always too low, and liver energy is usually too high. The typical excessive liver energy problem will begin when a person uses force to get what he desires. When he is denied what he wants, anger sets in. Internally the energy will expand and become volatile and active. The blood pressure may rise and the tendons and ligaments begin to tighten, causing the muscles to harden and tense. Soreness and pain will develop. The eyes may get bloodshot and bulge as if the excess energy is pushing them out. The vision will sometimes get blurred, and the voice will always have an angry undertone. The facial expression will often have an angry look. It's as if the sufferer of excess liver energy is "spring loaded" and ready to burst. People in this state commonly turn to alcohol to relieve pressure and relax the body. This will work for a while, but since alcohol is bad for the liver, the liver will eventually become even more active. An overactive liver will fuel anger, and its owner won't necessarily know if the alcohol caused the anger or the anger fueled the taste for alcohol. The volatile energy may cause pressure to build up in specific spots: if a person thinks too much, pressure may build in his head, causing headaches and migraines. He may also feel dizziness, nausea, and pain behind the eyes.

The solution for this condition is simple relaxation—let go. One must know when to retreat and surrender, and anger must be counteracted with forgiveness. Anger can also be released with the Liver Healing Sound (page 100). Volatile energy needs to be calmed with stillness and cooled with Heavenly Energy Meditation (page 157). The pent-up energy may also be released with cleansing, and tendons and muscles may be loosened and kept flexible with stretching exercises.

LIVER ENERGY IMBALANCES

Insufficient Liver Energy	General Liver Ailments	Excess Liver Energy
Blurry vision	Eye pain	High blood pressure
Weak joints		Tightness of the tendons and ligaments
Chipped and cracked nails		Muscle spasms and cramps
		Stiff arms and legs
		Blurry vision
		Bloodshot eyes
		Migraines and headaches
		Nausea
		Vertigo
		Dizziness
		Hypertension

SOLUTIONS FOR INSUFFICIENT LIVER ENERGY

1. **Eye Massage (page 130).** This exercise is good for many eye problems. It will relax the muscles around the eye, promoting better circulation, relieve pain and pressure around the eye, and restore clarity of vision.

SOLUTIONS FOR GENERAL LIVER AILMENTS

1. **Wood Exercise (page 77).** This is good for your daily routine and will help regulate and balance the flow of blood.
2. **Heavenly Energy Meditation (page 157).** This meditation will cool the body and help release pent-up hot energy, clearing the entire body. It will also replace, restore, and purify energy.

SOLUTIONS FOR EXCESS LIVER ENERGY

1. **Temple Massage (page 130).** Headaches are often caused by energy accumulating in the head. This massage is very good for headaches, since it helps break up stagnant energy trapped in the head and restore clear and even energy flow.
2. **Shoulder Massage (page 131).** A lot of tension can build up from stress and anger, and it often collects in the neck and shoulders. This massage can provide instant relief in the tendons, ligaments, and muscles as well. This massage will release pressure while calming the mind and emotions.
3. **Opening the Gates (pages 45–50).** These are stretching exercises that will loosen the joints and tendons while relaxing the body.
4. **Liver Healing Sound (page 100).** Liver Healing Sound will help release any anger that may have built up. This practice can lower blood pressure, and is also particularly good when overheating occurs.
5. **Joining the Valley Point (page 138).** This point is good for relieving spasms and headaches, and should help calm the mind and relieve pain in the arms and shoulders.

6. **Great Rushing Point (page 139).** This point is good for relieving spasms and headaches and releasing anger, frustration, and stress. It is particularly effective for relieving facial tension when it is done before or after the Joining the Valley Point.

7. **Three Yin Crossing (page 137).** This practice promotes the smooth functioning of the liver, smooth blood flow, and it relieves pain. It also helps regulate the uterus, menstruation, and most gynecological functions.

HEART ENERGY IMBALANCES AND SOLUTIONS

Instant gratification, excitement, and constant stimuli are all very important and prevalent in modern life. Excitement is fun, but overexcitement, constant thrill, and disappointment can lead to an energy imbalance in the heart. The energy of the heart reacts like fire. The heart energy can either radiate brightly or be squelched out like wet embers. A flamboyant and roller-coaster lifestyle can lead to extreme fluctuations of the heart energy.

The lifestyle of a stockbroker may best typify how the heart energy loses its balance. The stockbroker must think quickly, handle pressure, gamble, and motivate and excite others. All of these actions cause the heart energy to heat up and become volatile. This is normally not a problem unto itself, but if it remains in constant flux, hot energy and pressure may build up. The stockbroker can quickly fill up with hot energy like a balloon pumped up with hot air, and find that she needs to vent this heat. She will crave cold foods to cool the body. Her mouth is always dry, so she consumes cold drinks constantly. She will talk incessantly to release excess energy, heat, and excitement. Sometimes, however, her excited talk can generate a nervous energy and agitation. The pressure and heat can build further. Her chest may become tight and painful. She may sweat a lot, or her skin may dry up. Her eyes become bloodshot, and her face always looks flushed and red. Her voice has a laughing tone to it, but as the blood pressure continues to rise sleeping becomes difficult, and she may become temperamental. While the liver person's anger is directed specifically, the fire person's anger is like a quick explosion directed at no one in particular. To deal with a high-pressure life the fire person will look for other forms of stimuli. It's like trading one high for another but never wanting to come down. Her high-energy work will create a high-energy personal life. Sex, drugs, and burning the candle at both ends may become prevalent. The fire person will inevitably crash as the energy burns itself out; whereupon the fire person will withdraw and become depressed. Her circulation may weaken, and her complexion may become pale. Her blood pressure is low, and instead of being constantly hot she is now constantly cold. Since the heart is connected to the circulatory system, ailments related to the heart and veins such as varicose veins and clogged arteries may arise.

The person with heart energy imbalances often just needs to slow down. She needs to understand that less is more. If her condition is an excess of heart energy, then she needs to cool down, vent, and cleanse. If, on the other hand, she is lacking heart energy then she needs to stimulate and add energy to the system. In general she needs to increase circulation throughout the body and even to the hands and feet. Increased circulation can alleviate pressure and vent excessive heat, or it can help restore and build energy when there is a deficiency.

HEART ENERGY IMBALANCES

Insufficient Heart Energy	General Heart Ailments	Excess Heart Energy
Varicose veins	Poor circulation	High blood pressure
Cold hands and feet	Heart problems	Insomnia
Always cold	Chest pain	
Low blood pressure	Clogged arteries	Fast or forceful pulse and heartbeat
		Body overheats
Pale complexion		Red face
Slow or weak pulse and heartbeat		Sensations down arm
		Profuse sweating
		Shortness of breath
		Heart palpitations

SOLUTIONS FOR INSUFFICIENT HEART ENERGY

1. **Triple Heater Healing Sound (page 102).** This practice will increase overall body energy, increase body warmth, and regulate blood pressure.
2. **Kidney Massage (page 128).** This massage will invigorate the energy of the kidneys, which will in turn counterbalance the energy of the heart. This massage will also warm the body and improve circulation.
3. **Bubbling Spring Point (page 136).** This practice will regulate the energy in the kidneys and the heart while balancing body temperature.

SOLUTIONS FOR GENERAL HEART AILMENTS

1. **Fire Exercise (page 79).** This should be your first approach to a troubled heart. This exercise will balance the energy of the heart and improve circulation.
2. **Heart Healing Sound (page 100).** This practice is appropriate if you are feeling restless, overexcited, or nervous.
3. **Still Meditation (page 33).** This meditation will calm you down.
4. **Heart Massage (page 131).** This massage is particularly good for a tight chest or chest pain. This exercise, done in conjunction with the Heart Healing Sound, either before or after, is an excellent way to balance the heart energy.
5. **Immortal Embracing Post (page 149).** This practice helps restore energy to the chest area. This exercise works best if you have been doing the program for four months or more.

SOLUTIONS FOR EXCESS HEART ENERGY

1. **Cleansing Exercises (page 55).** These exercises will release the excess energy and heat that frequently cause insomnia. They will also regulate blood pressure.
2. **Heavenly Energy Meditation (page 157).** This practice will cool the body.
3. **Inner Gate Point (page 138).** This practice is particularly good for insomnia.
4. **Bubbling Spring Point (page 136).** This practice is good for venting any excess heat and energy. It is good for insomnia and headaches.

Spleen Energy Imbalances
and Solutions

According to traditional Chinese medicine, the function of the spleen is to convert food into energy. Consequently, problems involving spleen energy have to do with food, the digestive system, and elimination. All of the different elemental personalities have a unique way of losing balance and creating problems. When the wood type person is frustrated, he generates a lot of anger. When the fire type person is stressed she burns a lot of energy. When the earth type person is under duress, he directs his troubles inward. Like a doting mother, he harbors and internalizes problems because he feels he can handle it all. It is not surprising that the emotion associated with the earth person and the spleen is worry.

Worry is at the core of the typical spleen problem. To alleviate stress and worry, an earth person will resort to overeating, irregular eating habits, and a poor diet. Overeating will stress and slow the digestive system. Eating at strange or late hours may cause food to just sit in the stomach. Poor diets, usually lacking in fiber, allow food to stay in the digestive system for too long. The slowing and stagnation in the digestive system will cause the energy of the spleen and stomach to slow down and get sluggish. The earth person then gets gas, his stomach bloats, and he always feels full. He may also retain water and feel bogged down. The earth person will try to eat less frequently to compensate, but when he does eat, he tends to eat too much because he feels like he has starved himself. Overeating stresses the digestive system, which causes it to slow down even more. As a result the nutrients from the food will not be absorbed as efficiently, and the earth person's energy level will drop from lack of nutrition. He will begin to crave sweets and fatty foods for gratification and instant energy. He will gain weight as the sluggish digestive system causes more of the food to turn to fat. His mind will begin to think too much about his weight problem, and as worry sets in his digestive system is slowed even more. He will then start to eat a lot of salad, fruits, and raw vegetables to lose weight. From a Chinese perspective, these are all "cold" foods, and a diet that has too much cold food slows down the digestive system. With the spleen energy out of balance, the person is susceptible to other problems such as constipation, diarrhea, diabetes, ulcers, and hypoglycemia. Finally, as the spleen energy is related to the muscles, the muscles may lose tone and feel weak.

The solution to any spleen condition is first and foremost good eating habits. The earth person needs to eat a balanced diet. Fiber is good but too many raw foods are too "cold" and slow down digestion. It is advised that the earth person eat raw fruit but cooked vegetables, along with nourishment from all of the basic food groups. Cooking vegetables changes their energetic quality from cold to warm. From a Chinese perspective cooked vegetables are more balanced and conducive to digestion. One should eat small amounts frequently as opposed to eating large amounts infrequently, a practice that will keep the digestive system active and clear. The earth person should not eat late at night, since the food will tend to stay in the system for too long. The Chi Kung solutions for spleen imbalances are usually the same whether the problem is one of excess energy or deficiency. This is because the problem is almost always one of stagnation, which is caused both by deficient and excess energy. The Stomach Massage (page 132) is the single most effective solution for spleen energy and weight gain problems. This exercise will stimulate energy flow in the stomach while relieving muscular tension in the abdomen.

SPLEEN ENERGY IMBALANCES

Insufficient Spleen Energy	General Spleen Ailments	Excess Spleen Energy
Lack of energy	Discomfort in the stomach	Acid indigestion
Malnutrition	Weight problem	Constipation
Diabetes	Hypoglycemia	Flatulence
Allergies	Sugar cravings	Ulcers
Shakiness	Bloating in stomach	Excessive hunger
Diarrhea	Sluggish digestion	Water retention
Tooth decay		Irregular bowel movement and urination
Bleeding gums		
Lack of muscle tone		
Weak abdominal muscles		Pain in abdominal region
		Tender gums
		Presence of phlegm in nose and throat

SOLUTIONS FOR INSUFFICIENT SPLEEN ENERGY

All of the insufficiency solutions are in the general section.

SOLUTIONS FOR GENERAL SPLEEN AILMENTS

1. **Earth Exercise (page 80).** This exercise should be part of your daily routine. It will not only restore energy in the spleen but also clear stagnant energy from the spleen.
2. **Stomach Massage (page 132).** This is a great exercise for weight loss. It is also good for constipation, diarrhea, bloating, sluggish digestion, and upset stomach.
3. **Three Yin Crossing Point (page 137).** This point will resolve water retention, relieve pain in the lower abdominal region, and boost sluggish digestion.

4. **Three Mile Point (page 136).** This practice will strengthen the spleen and is good for assimilating nutrition from food and for promoting elimination.

5. **Holding the Ball (page 149).** This exercise can greatly increase energy in the stomach and spleen. It is a more advanced exercise that is very effective when done after doing the Stomach Massage (page 130).

SOLUTIONS FOR EXCESS SPLEEN ENERGY

1. **Spleen Healing Sound (page 101).** This practice is appropriate if you have a lot on your mind. It can quickly break up stagnant energy and stimulate digestion. This exercise is also particularly helpful in releasing emotional anxiety, which often leads to ulcers.

2. **Bubbling Spring Point (page 136).** This practice is very good for relieving severe anxiety.

LUNG ENERGY IMBALANCES AND SOLUTIONS

According to the beliefs of traditional Chinese medicine the body can develop illness either internally, from emotional and mental stress, or externally, via the invasion of outside elements. It is believed that wind, heat, cold, dryness, and dampness can enter the body and disrupt the balance of the internal ecosystem. When the internal ecosystem is out of balance—if there is too much heat, for instance—the body will suffer. Pathogens can also invade the body causing illness. Everyone has a layer of energy that surrounds the body, protecting us from these invasions. The Chinese call it the "Wei Chi." The Wei Chi emanates from the body like a bubble and keeps the elements, pathogens, and negative energy from entering the body. The Wei Chi can be built up very strong, and legend has it that the Wei Chi of certain Tai Chi and Chi Kung masters was so powerful that the force of the Wei Chi could physically push a person back. There are today masters known to be able to use their Wei Chi to push others without physically touching them. They simply extend their Wei Chi. It is not necessary, however, to develop the Wei Chi to this degree just to stay healthy.

The energy of the lungs directly controls the Wei Chi. If the lung energy is vibrant, the Wei Chi will be strong, and the body will be able to stave off infection. If the lung energy is stagnant, the Wei Chi will withdraw and shrink, and the body is susceptible to illness. The emotion associated with the lungs is grief. It is very common for the lung energy to stagnate when someone experiences the loss of a loved one or another such deep disappointment. The person's Wei Chi will weaken, and before long he may catch a cold, the flu, or some other virus. Allergies may also arise. The Wei Chi nourishes the outer portion of the body, namely the skin and hair. When lung energy is vibrant, the skin and hair will shine. When lung energy is out of balance, the skin and hair will become dry and coarse. The skin may also become overly sensitive. The Wei Chi also affects the pores and, in general, the relationship of the body to the outside. When lung energy is stagnant the person may perspire profusely, or he may perspire at night when he's sleep. The entire respiratory system is also connected to the lung energy. Unbalanced lung energy may congest the sinuses, cause sinus headaches, and lead to a dry cough. The chest may feel tight, and chest pain may develop. Weak lung energy will make breathing difficult, and as a result a person may develop a lack of endurance.

The solution for lung problems is to breathe deeply and fully. Correct breathing, along with a focused mind and good posture, is the basis of Chi Kung. Sinking the breath deep into the lungs to fully expand the lungs will restore energy and induce energy circulation. Do not force the expansion of the lungs, but focus your awareness on the abdomen. Let the abdomen expand when you inhale and contract when you exhale. Also it is good to try to get fresh air. If it is possible, practice Chi Kung outside in a park or anywhere with fresh, clean air. The morning air is particularly rejuvenating.

As we have already mentioned, grief is the cause for many lung energy problems. The Lung Healing Sound (page 101) is highly recommended after a disappointing and emotional separation or loss. It can offer instant relief and soothe the soul while releasing stagnant energy in the lungs. With the lungs it is sometimes difficult to discern whether there is a deficiency or an excess of energy since the symptoms of these conditions are sometimes similar. It is recommended that you spend more time with the general solutions. If you are confident that you know you have a deficiency or an excess, do the exercises that are fitting, but using the general solutions may also solve your problem.

LUNG ENERGY IMBALANCES

Insufficient Lung Energy	General Lung Ailments	Excess Lung Energy
Susceptible to colds and flus	Poor circulation	Chest pain and tightness
Lack of endurance	Chemical and food allergies	Coarse skin and hair
Weak respiration	Sinus congestion	Sinus headaches
Sensitive skin	Lung weakness	Lack of perspiration
Weak hair	Dry coughs	Stiff joints
Night sweating		
Oversensitivity to weather changes		

SOLUTIONS FOR INSUFFIENT LUNG ENERGY

1. **Lung Massage (page 132).** This exercise will help increase energy in the lungs and improve respiration.

SOLUTIONS FOR GENERAL LUNG AILMENTS

1. **Sinus Massage (page 132).** This practice is good if you have any sinus problems or a sinus headache.
2. **Metal Exercise (page 83).** All of the five element exercises are good for daily maintenance. The Metal-Lung Five Element Exercise will strengthen the immune system and help combat colds, flu, and allergies.
3. **Immortal Embracing Post (page 149).** This is an advanced exercise, but it can be effective for the beginner. It works best if you do the Metal-Lung Five Element Exercise beforehand.
4. **Joining the Valley Point (page 138).** This practice is good for clearing sinus congestion and headaches. It will also relieve tension and tightness in the joints of the shoulders and arms.

SOLUTIONS FOR EXCESS LUNG ENERGY

1. **Lung Healing Sound (page 101).** If you are experiencing sorrow and disappointment, do this exercise. It will also help relieve pain, tension, and tightness in the chest.

Gate of Life Prone Position—Lie on your back. Overlap the palms and place them under the Gate of Life point, which is on the spine, opposite the navel. The palms face the ground. With each breath feel the body release any tension and tightness. Feel the lower back relax and warm. Feel the warmth in the palms, and feel energy ascend out of the palms and into

the lower back. Feel the energy grow and fill into the kidneys. Feel the kidneys being stimulated and nourished. This exercise is very good for lower back pain and stiffness.

Kidney Massage (1–3 minutes)—Rub your hands together to create heat. Place your palms on the lower back. Rub the kidneys in a circular motion. Rub vigorously to warm the kidneys. Feel the muscles of the lower back relax and release tightness. Feel energy from the palms enter the kidneys. Feel the kidneys warm and fill with energy.

Horse Stance (1–5 minutes)—Stand with your legs wide apart. Bend your knees, pushing them out to the side slightly so that the knee is above the toes. Keep the lower back pushed in and roll the hips in and under. Keep the back straight. Let the torso sink into the hips. The more the thighs become parallel to the ground, the more intense and powerful the exercise will be. Place the back of the hands on the kidneys. Focus your mind on the lower abdomen. As the body heats, channel your energy to the kidneys. Feel the kidneys warm and fill up with energy. Try to relax and breathe deeply and evenly.

Beating and Drumming the Chi (3–5 minutes)—Stand comfortably with good posture. Inhale and imagine energy ascending from the perineum to the lower back and into the stomach. Exhale and imagine energy descending from the stomach to the front of the lower abdomen and back to the perineum. Visualize the energy as a spinning ball of light in the lower abdomen. Reinforce this imagery by guiding the energy with the fingers. Draw imaginary circles on the sides of the lower torso. Feel the energy passing through the tailbone, stomach, lower abdomen, and geni-

tals. Feel the whole area being rejuvenated and stimulated.

Eye Massage (1–3 minutes)—Rub the hands together until they get hot. Cup the palms and gently place them over the eyes. Feel the energy and warmth flow into the eyes. Feel the eyes being stimulated.

Temple Massage (1–3 minutes)—With the fingers, massage the temples in a circular motion. Massage clockwise or up the back and down the front. The major energy channels that flow through the head flow in

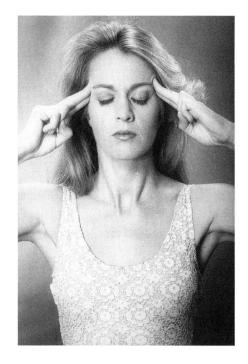

this direction, and the energy in the brain naturally flows in this direction, too. Imagine energy projecting from the fingers and into the head. Feel energy stagnation being broken up and released. Feel the flow of energy in the brain being stimulated. This exercise is very soothing for headaches.

Shoulder Massage (1–3 minutes)— With both hands grab the top of the shoulders or the trapezius muscles that support the neck. Knead the muscles and work out the tension and hardness. Breathe deeply and relax

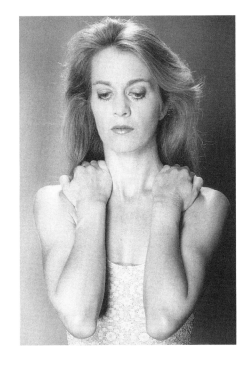

the body. Imagine dark energy and tension descending through the body and into the ground.

Heart Massage (1–3 minutes)—Place the palms on the upper part of the sternum. Press and make small circles with the palms. Relax and feel the tissues relax and release tension. Feel energy penetrating into the chest and heart region. If you want to increase energy because of an insufficiency, then rub faster. If you want to calm and sedate the heart region because you have excessive energy, then rub more slowly.

Stomach Massage (3–30 minutes)— Overlap your palms on your stomach. Rub circles on the lower abdomen clockwise for at least 36 revolutions and counterclockwise for 36 revolutions. You may vary the size of the circles from smaller to larger and then from larger to smaller. Imagine energy flowing from the palms into the body. Imagine you are gently stirring the stomach and intestines. If you have sluggish digestion or constipation, then only do *clockwise* circles. If you have diarrhea, then only do *counterclockwise* circles. This is an excellent exercise for weight loss because it stimulates the digestive system to work more efficiently.

Lung Massage (1–3 minutes)—Place your fingers just below the clavicles. Gently apply pressure with fingers. Massage the area just under the collarbone. Visualize energy extending from the fingers into the top of the lungs. Feel the lungs and the entire chest being stimulated and rejuvenated. Breathe deeply, fully, and evenly.

Sinus Massage (1–3 minutes)—With the fingers massage the upper cheek under the eyes. Proceed up the bridge of the nose and finish by rubbing the

occipital ridge above the eyebrows. Feel tightness and pressure leave the face and head. Feel stagnant energy and blockages being broken up and released. Imagine dark, hot energy drifting out of the head. Use your deep breathing to help you relax.

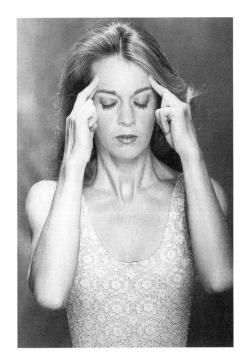

ENERGY POINTS

There is a network of rivers of energy that traverse the body. There are points within this system that are significant and easily accessible to the hands. Their locations are usually indentations and soft spots in between muscles, bones, and tendons. These areas are frequently tender and sensitive to the touch. Key points are often located where major rivers of energy flow near the surface of the body, where they intersect, or where they originate. The stimulation of these key points can greatly promote energy flow within a river of energy. If the point is an intersection point, then multiple rivers can be affected. The increase in energy flow can profoundly help the body to heal and alleviate a variety of problems.

The following exercises focus on a few of the most effective energy points of the body. Each point has a variety of functions that can combat certain ailments. For each point exercise, we teach a posture that makes it easy and comfortable to find and press a particular point. A stretch can also easily be done while holding energy points and good posture. While stretches are unrelated to the function of a given energy point, doing them will help relax the mind and body and make the exercise more enjoyable. All of the points given are symmetrical in that each has a counterpart on the opposite side of the body. For example, if a point is on a particular location in the left hand, then the same spot on the right hand is also an energy point with the same function. For the sake of space we only give the posture and location for points on one side. You may easily do the opposite side and enjoy the same benefit, but doing both sides is not necessary.

Joining the Valley Point.

When finding an energy point for the first time, remember that the point will be soft and tender. The place where it hurts when you apply a lot of pressure is usually the right spot. As you hold the point, focus your mind on the location of your ailment. If your ailment has no exact location, then focus on the organ to which the point corresponds. This organ is listed in parentheses for each point. Imagine energy pouring into the point and traveling to the ailment or organ. Visualize the energy alleviating the problem. See the tissues of the area in a perfectly healthy state. See the whole area vibrant and rejuvenated. Imagine dark and stagnant energy flowing out of the problem area and back to the energy point. Visualize the bad energy gushing out of the point. Remember to relax and breathe deeply throughout the exercise.

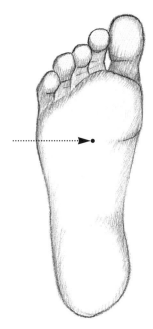

The Bubbling Spring Point.

Bubbling Spring Point (Kidney) (1–5 minutes)—Sit with your right leg forward. The left ankle rests on the right thigh. With your right thumb stimulate and apply gentle pressure to the "Bubbling Spring Point," which is located in the top, middle portion of the bottom of the foot, right where the arch begins. As you hold this point you can also bend forward, stretching the hamstring and hip. This point is called the Bubbling Spring Point because it is the place where the earth's energy rises into the body. Stimulating this point will decrease body heat, restore consciousness, balance the kidney energy, calm the mind, calm the heart energy, alleviate headaches, and reduce severe anxiety.

Three Mile Point (Stomach) (1–5 minutes)—Sit on the floor with both legs extended in front of you. On the outside of the leg about 2–3 inches below the middle of the kneecap, find the soft spot between the tibia and the fibia—the "Three Mile Point"—and press with the thumb. To stretch the hamstrings and calves, bend forward at the waist and pull the toes back. This point is called the Three Mile Point because it is said that you will have the energy to walk three miles after you stimulate this point. Stimulating this point will combat fatigue, promote digestion, relieve water retention, and balance the kidney energy.

Three Yin Crossing Point (Spleen) (1–5 minutes)—Sit with both legs extended in front of you. Slide the hands to the ankles. About 3 inches up from the ball of the ankle joint on the inside of the leg find the "Three Yin Crossing Point." Press with the thumb. If you straighten the knees and pull the toes back, you can stretch the calves and hamstrings. This point is aptly named the Three Yin Crossing

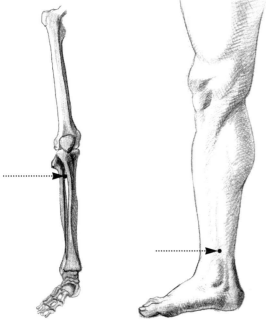

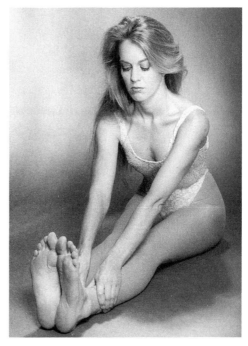

The Three Mile Point.   *The Three Yin Crossing Point.*

because it is the intersection of three main rivers of energy that feed the spleen, liver, and kidneys. Accordingly, pressing this point will balance the energy of the spleen, liver, and kidneys. It will also nourish the blood, regulate menstruation, alleviate gynecological problems, circulate the blood, help urination, relieve pain in general, relieve lethargy, and ease dizziness.

Joining the Valley Point (Large Intestine) (1–5 minutes)—Sit with the legs wide apart. Find the soft flesh on the back of the right hand between the thumb and index finger. Press with the thumb and index finger on the meaty part close to where the bones meet. You may lean forward to stretch the groin. This is the "Joining the Valley Point," and stimulating this point is particularly good for relieving a headache. This point will also balance the lung energy, clear the lungs and nasal congestion, fight colds and allergies, and relieve pain in the uterus and intestines. Pregnant women should not stimulate this point, as it is used to induce labor.

Inner Gate Point (Pericardium) (1–5 minutes)—Sit with the legs wide apart, as in Joining the Valley Point. Place

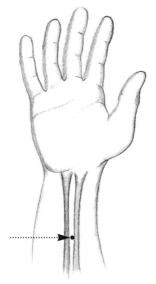

The Inner Gate Point.

your left thumb on the inside and middle of the right wrist. About 2 inches below where the wrist meets the hand, feel for the valley between the tendons. This is the "Inner Gate Point." Press gently with the thumb. If you want to stretch the groin and hamstrings while stimulating the Inner Gate Point, merely widen the legs and bend forward at the waist. This point will balance the energy of the heart, promote sleep, open the chest, regulate the heart, chi, and blood, reduce anxiety and irritability, relieve nausea and vomiting, and calm the mind.

Great Rushing Point (Liver) (1–5 minutes)—Sit with the knees out with the bottoms of the feet touching. On the top of the foot find the valley between the big toe and next largest toe. At about 2 to 3 inches down from the tip of the big toe, feel for a natural depression. Press the "Great Rushing Point" with the middle and index fingers on both feet. If you pull the knees to the ground and bend forward, you can also stretch the groin. Stimulating this point will balance and calm the energy of the liver, relieve headaches, reduce muscle cramps and contractions, and relieve anger and frustration. This exercise is very good for tense and nervous people.

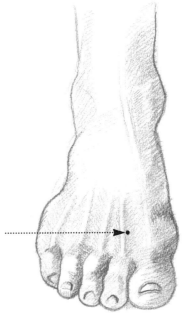

The Great Rushing Point.

Month Five

Integration

Holding the Ball.

The exercises taught thus far can thoroughly make the body strong and healthy. These exercises, or at least the principles of these exercises, are commonly practiced in China and cover the basics of Chi Kung. The exercises of month five are more advanced and intense and are usually only practiced by experienced Chi Kung students, martial artists, and energetic healers. These exercises are sometimes taught earlier because of their effectiveness, but they work best after you have spent some time building and cleansing your chi. The Seas of Energy exercises intensify and increase the energy in the main centers that rest in the lower abdomen, chest, and head. These seas of energy serve as storage centers for the body's internal energy. Like a battery that powers a machine, the energy centers provide the fuel that keeps the body vibrant and alive.

Week Seventeen (New: Opening the Heavenly Eye)

Minimum Practice **(5 minutes)**	Option 1: Still Meditation (5 minutes) Option 2: Back Stretches and Opening the Gates (5 minutes) Option 3: Cleansing Exercises (5 minutes) Option 4: Small Orbit Exercise (5 minutes)

Week Seventeen (New: Opening the Heavenly Eye) (*cont'd*)

Short Program **(25 minutes)**	Option 1: Still Meditation (5–10 minutes) Back Stretches and Opening the Gates (5–10 minutes) Cleansing Exercises (5 minutes) Small Orbit Exercise (5–10 minutes) Option 2: Still Meditation (5 minutes) Cleansing Exercises (5 minutes) Five Element Exercises (5–10 minutes) **Opening the Heavenly Eye (5–10 minutes)**
Long Program **(35–45 minutes)**	Still Meditation (5–10 minutes) Back Stretches and Opening the Gates (5–10 minutes) Cleansing Exercises (5 minutes) Small Orbit Exercise (5–10 minutes) Five Element Exercises (5–10 minutes) **Opening the Heavenly Eye (10–15 minutes)**

Week Eighteen (New: Immortal Embracing Post)

Minimum Practice **Short Program** **(25 minutes)**	(same as above) Option 1: (same as above) Option 2: Still Meditation (5–10 minutes) Cleansing Exercises (5 minutes) Five Element Exercises (5–10 minutes) **Immortal Embracing Post (5–10 minutes)**
Long Program **(35–45 minutes)**	Still Meditation (5–10 minutes) Back Stretches and Opening the Gates (5–10 minutes) Cleansing Exercises (5 minutes) Small Orbit Exercise (5–10 minutes) Five Element Exercises (5–10 minutes) **Immortal Embracing Post (10–15 minutes)**

Week Nineteen (New: Holding the Ball)

Minimum Practice **Short Program** **(25 minutes)**	(same as above) Option 1: (same as above) Option 2: Still Meditation (5–10 minutes) Cleansing Exercises (5 minutes) Five Element Exercises (5–10 minutes) **Holding the Ball (5–10 minutes)**

Long Program (35–45 minutes)	Still Meditation (5–10 minutes) Back Stretches and Opening the Gates (5–10 minutes) Cleansing Exercises (5 minutes) Small Orbit Exercise (5–10 minutes) Five Element Exercises (5–10 minutes) **Holding the Ball (10–15 minutes)**

Week Twenty (Review Seas of Energy Excercises)

Minimum Practice **Short Program** **(25 minutes)**	(same as above) Option 1: (same as above) Option 2: Still Meditation (5 minutes) Cleansing Exercises (5 minutes) Five Element Exercises (5 minutes) **Seas of Energy Exercises—All Three (10 minutes)**
Long Program **(35–45 minutes)**	Still Meditation (5–10 minutes) Back Stretches and Opening the Gates (5–10 minutes) Cleansing Exercises (5 minutes) Small Orbit Exercise (5–10 minutes) Five Element Exercises (5–10 minutes) **Seas of Energy Exercises—All Three (10–15 minutes)**

THE SEAS OF ENERGY EXERCISES

Why is the sea king of a hundred streams?
Because it lies below them.
Therefore it is the king of a hundred streams.
　　　　　　　　　　　　　　　—Lao Tsu

The Seas of Energy, or tan tiens.

Up to now we have been working the meridians, which are analogous to rivers of energy, and the internal organs, which reside in pools or lakes of energy. We are now going to concentrate on the "tan tiens," or "Seas of Energy." There are three tan tiens, and they all rest on the "Tai Chi Pole," or "center core," which runs from the crown of the head to the perineum, down the inside and center of the body. The lower tan tien is located in the abdomen, and its core is two inches below the navel. The middle tan tien resides in the chest, and its nucleus is even with the middle of the sternum. The upper tan tien is centered in the middle of the head (see diagram).

All of the rivers and lakes of energy intersect, connect, and feed the Three Seas of Energy. The Three Seas serve as receptacles or storage areas for the chi. They can also serve as refineries or distilleries. If the energy in these seas is stimulated, intensified, and circulated, the energy is refined and distilled to a more pure, light, and vibrant state. When someone has health problems or emotional stress, the energy is very heavy and viscous like old motor oil or chunky like ice water. When someone is healthy and has inner peace, the energy is light, clean, and vibrant. The achievement of this more refined state is termed "opening" the tan tiens. The tan tiens need to be opened and activated just as the meridians must be unclogged and the organs need to be purified. The Sea of Energy Exercises will help you do this.

As each Sea of Energy, or energy center, opens, it affects a different aspect of one's being. The lower tan tien is associated with physical and sexual energy. When the lower tan tien opens and becomes vibrant, one feels physically strong, rejuvenated, youthful, and energetic. Fatigue fades away, and endurance increases. Physical sensitivity and awareness is heightened, and athletic performance is enhanced. The lake of energy that houses the kidneys is connected to the lower Sea of Energy. Stimulating the lower energy center will positively affect the kidneys. The kidney energy is like a battery that fuels the other remaining Yin organs and the overall energy of the body. The kidney energy also nourishes the genitals and is associated with sexual vitality. Because of this, stimulating the lower Sea of Energy will increase overall energy and sexual energy.

The middle tan tien is related to mental and emotional growth. When the middle tan tien opens, one becomes more expressive and creative, the emotions stabilize, thinking becomes clearer, the actions are more purposeful, and relationships improve. The heart, lungs, liver, and spleen are connected to the middle Sea of Energy. Emotional energy is attached to these main organs, along with the kidneys. When the energy of the middle energy center intensifies and refines, the organ energy is strengthened and purified. Negative, stuffed emotions are disseminated, and positive traits such as joy, love, and courage come forth. Free from blinding negative emotion, the mind begins to see more clearly. As a result you become mentally and emotionally vibrant.

The upper tan tien is connected with the development of the spirit. When the upper tan tien opens, you become less attached to triviality and pettiness. Values become less external, compassion and trust increase, and a happy and content feeling arises. You begin to cherish what you have and worry less about what you do not have. You feel more connected to your spiritual beliefs and values. Circulating the energy in the upper energy center stimulates the very important "crown point." The crown point is like a gateway or connection to higher energy. It is believed that creativity, healing powers, and Divine inspiration flow into the crown point in the form of Heavenly energy. The Heavenly energy also has a cooling, soothing, and therapeutic effect on the mind and body. Stimulating and refining the energy in the upper tan tien will help open the crown point. A greater connection to one's spirituality may soon arise as a result.

Be sure to finish these exercises with Pulling Down the Heavens (page 59).

Opening the Heavenly Eye—Stand or sit with the feet a little wider than shoulder-width apart. The hips roll in and under. The back is straight. The chin is tucked in, gently elongating the neck. Lift the hands up to eye level. Let the elbows drop to shoulder level. Point the middle of the palms to the "third eye," or the midpoint between the eyebrows. Relax the body and sink your breathing. Imagine you are standing or sitting in water up to the level of the collarbone. Feel

the arms and elbows float on the water's surface. Relax the mind and let go of any worry or stress. Now visualize energy extending from the middle of the palms into the third eye. Feel the energy "tingle" in the forehead and brain. Feel the upper energy center being stimulated and cooled.

Immortal Embracing Post—Stand or sit comfortably in a posture exactly like the Opening the Heavenly Eye exercise. Bring the hands down to heart level. The palms face the body, the fingers point at each other. Imagine you are embracing a post. The fingers are spread, extended but relaxed. The elbows are out and the shoulders droop. Imagine you are in water up to chest level. Feel the water support the weight of the arms. Imagine your whole body floating. Relax and deepen your breathing. Visualize energy extending from the middle of the palms into the sternum. Feel the chest being opened and cleared. Feel the middle energy center being rejuvenated and enlivened.

Holding the Ball—Stand or sit comfortably with proper posture. Lower the hands to hip level. The palms face the body, and the fingers point at each other. The elbows are out. Imagine

you are embracing a large ball. Imagine you are standing or sitting in water at waist level. Relax the shoulders. Relax the entire body and feel the water helping you support the ball. The muscles should feel as if they are drooping and hanging from the bones. Now visualize energy projecting from the middle of the palms into the abdomen, two inches below the navel. Feel the abdomen relax and fill up. Feel the lower energy center being activated and heated.

SEAS OF ENERGY SENSATIONS

These exercises can be very intense, so you may generate a lot of heat. Remember to cool the body following these exercises with at least three repetitions of Pulling Down the Heavens. You may also tremble and shake, sensations caused by the clearing and breaking of chi blockages. You may feel a vibration or resonance throughout the body. You may even feel this in the bones. This is a sign of advanced progress, so in this case you should consult a Chi Kung teacher. Because you are also detoxing, with these exercises you may also feel a little nausea. You may become irritable and emotionally and mentally confused for a short time. You may also feel weak in the muscles and throughout the body. This is actually a sign that you are progressing and releasing negative energy. If the feeling persists for more than three days, then slow down.

Holding the Ball—Stimulating and opening the lower tan tien affects a person on the physical level. You may experience increased vitality and sexual energy, fullness and heat in the abdomen, vibration in the hands, and warmth in the kidneys. Your digestive system may feel stronger, and your endurance may increase. You may feel a renewed self-confidence and an overall feeling of physical well-being.

Immortal Embracing Post—Opening the middle tan tien will affect you mentally and emotionally. You may feel an actual "opening feeling" in the chest. You may experience a light, joyous, almost euphoric feeling. Emotional sensitivity may significantly increase, and you may also begin to let go of the ego and become more compassionate. Your thoughts will often become clearer and your emotions will balance. When the middle tan tien opens, this sometimes allows all three tan tiens to connect. You may develop a sense of connectedness and wholeness.

Opening the Heavenly Eye—Activating the upper tan tien influences you on a spiritual level. You may see a white light and/or a flashing light. You may feel a rainlike energy trickling down through the body—a quite pleasurable sensation. Some have experienced a feeling of timelessness, while others feel as if their body, thoughts, and emotions are "thinning" and disappearing. You may feel a stronger connection with God, the Divine, the universe, the energy of the stars, and/or a general strengthening of faith. You may notice a synchronicity in people and events. People whom you have forgiven in your heart may reappear in your life. Solutions may seem to just unfold before you.

Month Six

Awareness

The Lung Exercise.

All of the exercises presented thus far have concentrated on the "self." Centering on the self alone can lead to self-centeredness, which can trivialize everything you have just learned. The exercises of month six expand consciousness and awareness outside the body. The Heavenly Energy Meditation allows you to connect and experience the energy from the environment. The Loving Kindness Meditation is designed to encourage selfless love and compassion.

You have been presented with a variety of Chi Kung practices. You may have acquired preferences for some exercises over others, and now you can easily customize your own program. We highly recommend that you always include Still Meditation and the Cleansing Exercises in your routine.

Weeks Twenty-One and Twenty-Two
(New: Heavenly Energy Meditation)

Minimum Practice (5 minutes)	Option 1: Still Meditation (5 minutes)
	Option 2: Back Stretches and Opening the Gates (5 minutes)
	Option 3: Cleansing Exercises (5 minutes)
	Option 4: Small Orbit Exercise (5 minutes)

Weeks Twenty-One and Twenty-Two
(New: Heavenly Energy Meditation) (*cont'd*)

Short Program **(25 minutes)**	Option 1: Still Meditation (5–10 minutes) Back Stretches and Opening the Gates (5–10 minutes) Cleansing Exercises (5 minutes) Small Orbit Exercise (5–10 minutes) Option 2: Still Meditation (5 minutes) Cleansing Exercises (5 minutes) Five Element Exercises (5 minutes) Seas of Energy Exercises (5 minutes) **Heavenly Energy Meditation (5 minutes)**
Long Program **(35–45 minutes)**	Still Meditation (5–10 minutes) Back Stretches and Opening the Gates (5–10 minutes) Cleansing Exercises (5 minutes) Small Orbit Exercise (5–10 minutes) Five Element Exercises (5–10 minutes) Seas of Energy Exercises (5–10 minutes) **Heavenly Energy Meditation (5 minutes)**

Weeks Twenty-Three and Twenty-Four
(New: Loving Kindness Meditation)

Minimum Practice **Short Program** **(25 minutes)**	(same as above) Option 1: (same as above) Option 2: Still Meditation (5 minutes) Cleansing Exercises (5 minutes) Seas of Energy Exercises (5 minutes) Heavenly Energy Meditation (5 minutes) **Loving Kindness Meditation (5 minutes)**
Long Program **(40–45 minutes)**	Still Meditation (5–10 minutes) Back Stretches and Opening the Gates (5–10 minutes) Cleansing Exercises (5 minutes) Small Orbit Exercise (5 minutes) Five Element Exercises (5 minutes) Seas of Energy Exercises (5 minutes) Heavenly Energy Meditation (5 minutes) **Loving Kindness Meditation (5 minutes)**

Heavenly Energy Meditation

Hence it is said:
The bright path seems dim;
Going forward seems like retreat;
The easy way seems hard;
The highest Virtue seems empty;
Great purity seems sullied;
A wealth of Virtue seems inadequate;
The strength of Virtue seems frail;
Real Virtue seems unreal;
The perfect square has no corners;
Great talents ripen late;
The highest notes are hard to hear;
The greatest form has no shape.
The Tao is hidden and without name.
The Tao alone nourishes and brings everything to fulfillment.

—Lao Tsu

Developing energy does not necessarily balance a person physically, mentally, emotionally, and spiritually. It is not uncommon for a person to be highly developed in one area but underdeveloped in others. One who is physically developed but emotionally and spiritually weak can be abusive and destructive. One who is emotionally and mentally open but spiritually closed can be manipulative and controlling. One who is spiritually connected but emotionally repressed may verbalize good intent but never allow good intentions to transform into action. It is important to cultivate all aspects of being as equally as possible. The Sea of Energy Exercises you have learned are good for refining the energy in the three tan tiens individually. The Heavenly Energy Meditation will help fuse and connect the three Seas of Energy together, thereby developing the person more evenly.

As energy refines and distills, the body becomes healthier, and the mind becomes clearer. The distillation of the energy is analogous to the different states of water. When you are sick, the energy is like ice water. The energy is filled with blockages that are similar to chunks of ice slowing the flow. As you become healthier, the ice blockages melt, allowing for smooth and steady energy flow. As you become more vibrant and glowing, the water or energy becomes more like steam. Energy in a steamlike state is more powerful than energy in a waterlike state, but it is also gentler, lighter, and softer. As the energy continues to refine, the borders that delineate the three Seas of Energy become less apparent. This refinement of the energy along with the Heavenly Energy Meditation will make the three seas become more like one great ocean. When this union takes place, you will become balanced and connected physically, mentally, emotionally, and spiritually. Each level of your existence will work in accord.

Continued refinement will make the energy of the ocean even lighter and clearer. Before long, the ocean becomes clear enough to reveal a column of light. This column of light is called the center core or Tai Chi Pole, and it runs from the crown point to the perineum. The center core is always present no matter what your state of energy is, but the refinement of the energy allows the Seas of Energy to match its subtlety. Because the quality of the energies is now similar, the Seas of Energy and the center core can become one. It is believed that the center core holds the true essence or soul of a person. Who we are energetically manifests in the middle column of the body—our energetic bodies emanate out from the center core. Our deepest thoughts, beliefs, and innate goodness are part of this energetic core. There is a Chinese belief that the physical body will die but the center core will carry on. It is also believed that we hold on to masks and veils that serve to muddle and hide our center core. Ego, fear, and self-hatred are the fabric of these masks and veils. Our center core houses the most beautiful, pure, and endearing part of our inner nature, yet we choose to cover it up.

Distilling and refining the energy with the Seas of Energy Exercises and doing the Heavenly Energy Meditation will put you in touch with your center core. Letting go of fear, hate, and ego will dissolve the blanket of negatives that surround the center core.

The center core also needs to be connected to heavenly energy from above and earthly energy from the ground. The Chinese believe that there are three realms of energy: the heavenly realm, the earthly realm, and the human realm. The heavenly realm is the energy emanating from the cosmos, including the energy of the moon, sun, and stars. The earthly realm is the energy from the environment, which includes the energy of the air, ground, vegetation, water, and so forth. The human realm is comprised of energy within the body. The ancients found that energy from all three realms can be utilized to enhance your existence. To reach higher levels of ability with Chi Kung you have to get in tune with all three realms.

The earth energy is used frequently by martial artists to add stability and power to their movements. When you stand with proper posture, with the lower back pushed out and the hips rolled in and under, the feet will press firmly against the ground. This adjustment serves to ground the human energy to the energy of the earth. The energy of the earth can be drawn into the body like roots soaking up water. When this occurs your body and the earth are like two magnets stuck together, and your body is strengthened by drawing on this earth energy. The Heavenly Energy Meditation, along with the proper body posture, will establish this energetic union between earth and man.

The energy from the heavenly realm is tapped by Chi Kung healers to catalyze healing in a patient. The Chi Kung healers, through visualization and strength of will, will pull the heavenly energy into his body and center core, then project the energy from his center core, out of his body and into the patient. This heavenly energy is not only used for healing; it can also be used to rejuvenate the body and inspire the mind. This energy flows into the crown point, energizes the body, and connects with the body's energy core. It is believed that the intelligence of the universe, divine inspiration, creativity, and compassion come to us in the form of this energy. The Heavenly Energy Meditation will allow you to tap into these gifts from the heavens. Not only is the body reinforced but so is your center core, or soul.

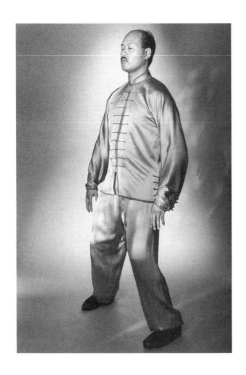

Wu Chi Position—Assume either a standing, sitting, or prone meditation position. Maintain good posture and gently close the eyes. Deepen and slow your breathing. Relax your body. Feel your muscles melt and your tension release. Relax your mind, letting go of any anger, worry, or sadness. Feel the weight of your body sink into the ground. Imagine roots growing from the bottoms of the feet down 20 feet into the ground.

Imagine a white liquid energy pouring from the heavens into the top of your head. Feel the energy tingle as it fills the head and upper Sea of Energy center or tan tien. Feel the energy enliven the tissues of the brain, face, and neck. The cool white energy overflows from the head and neck and begins to fill up the chest and middle Sea of Energy. Feel the heart and lungs being stimulated and the chest opening and clearing. The energy spills into the arms and hands and all the way to the fingertips. The energy continues to pour in, permeating the stomach, abdomen, and lower Sea of Energy. Feel the energy swirl around and clean and stimulate the kidneys, liver, spleen, bladder, gallbladder, and intestines. The white energy flows and expands into the legs. Feel the energy relax and strengthen the thighs, knees, calves, and feet. The energy descends into your roots, down into the ground. Imagine any energy blockages or dark energy washing away into the earth.

Feel the heavenly white energy continually pouring into the top of your head. Feel this white energy feed and strengthen the three Seas of Energy, or tan tiens. See the energy centers as radiant balls of bright light in the head, chest, and abdomen. The light pulsates and grows brighter. Finally the three Seas of Energy merge and become one. This union becomes a bright white column in the center of the body. The light column, or center core, begins to radiate outward through the pores of the skin and away from the body. The glow forms a protective shield as if it were a force field or bubble surrounding the body. The bubble keeps filling with energy, and the air becomes thicker. Relax and feel the pulsing energy. Allow the energy to slowly contract into the lower energy center. Feel the energy settle and the pulsing dissipate. Let heat and resonance leave the body. Slowly open your eyes. Perform three repetitions of Pulling Down the Heavens (page 59).

*L*OVING KINDNESS MEDITATION

Heaven and earth last forever.
Why do heaven and earth last forever?
They are unborn,
So ever living.
The sage stays behind. Thus he is ahead.
He is detached. Thus at one with all.
Through selfless action, he attains fulfillment.

—Lao Tsu

At this point you are five and a half months into the program. Now is a good time to revisit the questionnaire. Turn back to page 14 and photocopy the questionnaire. Answer the questions again, then pull out the original questionnaire that you filled out at the beginning of the program and see if there are any marked differences. Whether you feel there are or not, you are to be congratulated. You have shown discipline, concentration, faith, and an open mind. You had to have had moments where you felt like quitting, but you persevered. This program is about taking full responsibility for your health and self-improvement, and this did not scare you off. You could have looked for a solution in a pill or taken any number of other easy ways out, but you chose not to.

One day a teacher and student were out gathering fruit. The student was instructed to climb a tree to grab a piece of fruit from a high limb. As he climbed the tree the student was extremely careful because one slip would mean a long, hard fall. The teacher was silent as he watched. The student successfully grabbed the fruit and descended the tree. When he neared the bottom of his climb the teacher started shouting, "Careful! Watch out! Careful!"

The student reached the ground safely and asked his teacher, "Why did you warn me only when I was almost finished?"

The teacher replied, "When you were high up you knew it was dangerous, so you were careful. When you got near the bottom you didn't think you would slip. This is when you need to be reminded."

Self-cultivation can be very empowering. People who have developed the chi can do wondrous things. Their bodies are strong and healthy, their emotions are stable, their minds are sharp, and their whole beings are centered. From this centeredness, however, self-centeredness can develop. Self-cultivation can become selfishness. Empowerment can become ego. This transformation can happen to anyone and happens all too often. In fact, it is very common for a person who enjoys success in Chi Kung to develop an inflated ego, in spite of his or her so-called spiritual development. People can grow to think highly of themselves because they have worked hard for their success. They can forget, however, that success is in the eye of the beholder, and that we are all dealt different challenges and resources.

The great people I have met never seem to want to talk about themselves. They are constantly talking about other people's plights, giving credit to others, and extending compassion wherever they are. Interestingly, traits radiated by the special ones are qualities attainable by anyone. The Loving Kindness Meditation can make one become more compassionate. It can change one's self-awareness into simple, elevated awareness.

The words of the Loving Kindness Meditation can be read aloud or silently. You can start by just thinking about loved ones and close friends and, as your mind relaxes, extend the focus to less well known people. You can also just focus on a person with whom you want to patch up a relationship. While the key is sincerity, to do this meditation without it is still better than not doing it at all. This meditation was written by the esteemed Buddhist monk Ven. B. Ananda Maitreya Thera.

Loving Kindness Meditation—Sit comfortably in either a Lotus position or in a chair position. Keep your back straight and relax your body. Breathe deeply and evenly. Read or say the following words:

 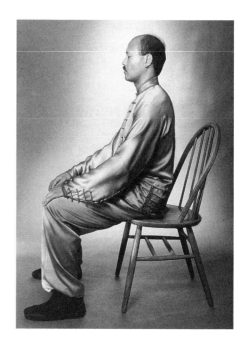

May I be well, happy, peaceful, and prosperous. May no harm come to me; may no difficulties come to me; may no problems come to me.

May I have patience, courage, understanding, and determination to meet and overcome inevitable difficulties, problems, and failures in life.

May my teachers be well, happy, peaceful, and prosperous. May no harm come to them; may no difficulties come to them; may no problems come to them.

May they have patience, courage, understanding, and determination to meet and overcome inevitable difficulties, problems, and failures in life.

May my parents be well, happy, peaceful, and prosperous.

May my relatives be well, happy, peaceful, and prosperous.

May my friends be well, happy, peaceful, and prosperous.

May all indifferent persons be well, happy, peaceful, and prosperous.

May my enemies be well, happy, peaceful, and prosperous.

May all living beings be well, happy, peaceful, and prosperous.

Whatever living beings there are,
timid, fearful, strong, confident,
long, great, or average,
short, small, or large,
seen or unseen,
living near or living far,
born or coming to birth,
May all beings be well and happy.
May we all be well and happy.
May I be well and happy.

May all beings be free from suffering. May all beings be free from fear. May all beings be free from grief. May all beings be well and happy.

May all beings be freed from all bondage and attain unsurpassed, supremely perfect Enlightenment.

Tools for Healthy Living

It is desired that you accept Chi Kung as a daily routine to maintain health and as a way to grow and develop as a person. The reason we hope for this is because we know that Chi Kung works. We've seen people get healthy using the exercises, and we've seen people grow and mature with the exercises. However, as with most things, only a minority of the people who are presented with Chi Kung will actually do it on a regular basis for a long time. This is the reality with any activity that demands willpower—Tai Chi, kung fu, meditation, weight lifting, jogging, karate, yoga, aerobics, healthy eating, you name it. This is understandable because only a few things in life will ever really capture our interest to the point that we want to dedicate time to them.

What we hope for is that everyone who has read this book will take at least one thing from this book and use it. You owe that to yourself if you have spent time and effort on this book. The exercises we have presented are just tools for healthy living that can be used when needed. They have been passed down for thousands of years because of their practicality and will, of necessity, continue to be passed down for thousands of years to come.

Recommended Reading, Viewing, and Listening

This is a beginning and basic book. It is designed to teach you the fundamentals of Chi Kung and give you a taste of the different ways energy is cultivated. You are encouraged to study further because there is so much more good information available about energy development, energetic healing, philosophy, and traditional Chinese medicine.

BOOKS

Effie Chow's *Miracle Healing from China—Chi Kung* (Coeur d'Alene, Idaho: Medi Press, 1994) is a good introduction to Chi Kung. She makes Chi Kung training very personable, accessible, and inspiring. She also gives encouraging accounts of people who have been cured with medical Chi Kung exercising.

Chi Kung—Cultivating Personal Energy (Shaftesbury, Dorset, UK: Element Books Limited, 1993) by James MacRitchie offers a very good bird's-eye view of Chi Kung. His presentation is clear, thoughtful, and well organized.

Between Heaven and Earth (New York: Ballantine, 1991), by Harriet Bienfield and Efrem Korngold, is a superbly written book that clearly explains how to use and understand traditional Chinese medicine. They successfully clarify some difficult concepts such that anyone can understand and use them.

The Book of Changes and the Unchanging Truth (Malibu, Calif.: The Shrine of the Eternal Breath of Tao, 1983), by Ni Hua Ching, is an excellent interpretation of this traditional classic. The book is used to help understand present and future events in one's life. The philosophy that can be learned from this book is filled with wisdom.

Lao Tsu's *Tao Te Ching*, translated by Gia-fu Feng and Jane English (New York: Vintage Books, 1989), is one of the most profound books ever written. All the poetry quoted throughout this book comes from the Tao Te Ching.

David Carradine's Tai Chi Workout (New York: Henry Holt, 1994), by David Carradine and David Nakahara, is our companion book. It is an introduction to the beautiful art of Tai Chi Chuan.

Advanced Chinese Medical Qi Gong: A Comprehensive Clinical Text (Pacific Grove, CA: International Qi Gong Institute, 1997) by Jerry Alan Johnson goes into great detail on how to develop the energy and how to heal with the energy. Johnson's work is always thorough as he has spent years gathering quality information while developing and honing his skill.

VIDEOS

All of the following recommended videos and audios are produced by PMN Distribution at 90 East Taylor St., San Jose, CA 95112, (408) 295-1842. One of the authors of this book owns this company, so the summaries are a bit biased. Trust us; these are all quality, well-produced products that can help you.

Chi Kung—The Healing Workout (1996). This program is solid, easy to follow, and very enjoyable. This is our best product. The imagery is startling as footage of waterfalls, sunsets, ocean waves, and time-lapse clouds are keyed into the background as the Chi Kung exercises are demonstrated.

Tai Chi—The Empowering Workout (1996). This is the companion tape to *Chi Kung—The Healing Workout*. This program also has the nature footage in the background. This tape gives the details that make Tai Chi an energy development art.

David Carradine's Tai Chi Workout (1987). This highly popular tape teaches a basic Tai Chi form. It also has a short Chi Kung routine.

David Carradine's Kung Fu Workout (1987). This program gives the basics of Kung Fu. Included is a very good stretching routine, stance training, kicking drills, and six short Shaolin exercise sets.

AUDIOCASSETTES AND COMPACT DISCS

Tai Chi Meditation—Life Force Breathing (1995). This CD or cassette is a guided meditation that increases overall energy. It presents a very easy way to begin to get in touch with internal energy while increasing body sensitivity. If you do not have time to work out, then listen to this tape before you sleep at night.

Tai Chi Meditation—Eight Direction Perception (1995). This CD or cassette is designed to increase perception and psychic abilities. This meditation is basically the advanced, long version of the Heavenly Energy Meditation given in this book. This meditation is more powerful than Life Force Breathing, but Life Force Breathing is more appropriate for beginners.

Future Plans

We are currently in production for a video that will serve as a companion to this book. The release date is set for January 1, 1998. You may order this video through PMN Distribution, 90 East Taylor Street, San Jose, CA 95112, 408-295-1842.

Biographies

❈

David Carradine, a successful film and television actor, gained international fame as the star of the popular television series *Kung Fu*. The original program is in syndication, and he is currently starring in the sequel, *Kung Fu: The Legend Continues*. He has authored several books on Chinese development arts and philosophy. He lives in Santa Clarista, California.

David Nakahara has studied Chinese martial, health, and healing arts for over twenty years and has taught them as well. He has produced, directed, and written several popular books and videos on the Chinese development arts.

Arnold E. Tayam, technical advisor for this book, is a Doctor of Chi Kung (China) as well as an instructor and practitioner of martial, medical, and spiritual Chi Kung. He is certified by several organizations including the International Chi Kung Institute of Monterey, California; Haidian University of Beijing, China; and the Universal Society of the Integral Way of Santa Monica, California.

Michael Lamont is a multitalented photographer whose work includes head shots, theater production, publicity stills, book jackets, and CD covers. A collection of his fine art photography will soon be published. He lives in Los Angeles, California.